The Power of Kindness
Empathy in a Traumatic World

Dr. James E. McReynolds
Minister of Joy to the World

Parson's Porch Books

The Power of Kindness: Empathy in a Traumatic World
ISBN: Softcover 978-1-960326-31-7
Copyright © 2023 by James E. McReynolds

Parson's Porch Books is an imprint of Parson's Porch *&* Company (PP*&*C) in Cleveland, Tennessee. PP*&*C is a self-funded charity which earns money by publishing books of noted authors, representing all genres. Its face and voice is **David Russell Tullock** who you can contact at: dtullock@parsonsporch.com.

Parson's Porch *&* Company *turns books into bread & milk* by sharing its profits with the poor.

www.parsonsporch.com

The Power of Kindness

Dedication

This book is dedicated to my grandson

Ethan Coffin

who has been a model for kindness

Contents

I shall pass through this life but once.
Any good, therefore that I can do,
Or any kindness I can show to any fellow creature,
Let me do it now.

Etienne de Grellet

Foreword

Dr. John R. Killinger

Somewhere in this book so sprawling with fresh ideas and thoughtful images, the author makes the statement that "Kindness is our natural state. The acting of kindness allows us to find a deep and profound connection."

"A deep and profound connection."

How true that is, and how important! We are not designed to live alone, to exist in isolation from other human beings. Most of us spend our lives trying to find meaningful connections with others, to become part of the whole of human existence. And, almost miraculously, when we are kind to others, we are making those connections.

I remember a man in one of my parishes who seemed to be the very soul of kindness. He told me once that he had decided several years earlier that he wanted in his lifetime to do a thousand kind deeds for others. I think he had already reached a number above three hundred.

He had one of the sunniest dispositions I have ever known, and everybody loved him. He seemed simply to exude kindness to everyone, wherever he went. I doubt if he ever met a stranger, because he was so immediately kind to everyone he encountered.

He was making that "deep and profound connection," all the time, wherever he went.

If God is love, as the Bible says, then love is at the very center of our existence. Every act of kindness connects us to that great love. Deeds of kindness consistently relate us to the heart of being itself. They Interswitch us with God and the universe and justify our existence on this planet.

I think I knew this instinctively, as a person who has always identified with the Christian faith and the ministry of Christ, but this book has made me more conscious of that wonderful relationship than I ever was before now. Having read it has caused me to remember it every time I do something thoughtful for one of my neighbors, or even when I contemplate reacting to the need of someone I have just met and don't really know very well.

This our "natural state," the author writes, the state where we truly belong, where our souls always have a place, where they find the real joy and fullness of their own existence. I never thought of that before reading the manuscript of this exceptional volume. I know that it is very true. I shall always be greatly indebted to James McReynolds for bringing it so forcefully to my attention.

He is indeed, as Dr. Norman Vincent Peale once anointed him as the Minister of Joy to the World.

John R. Killinger
Warrenton, Virginia

Chapter One

The Power of Kindness

Kindness is one of the most beautiful and most powerful forces that exists in the world today. Kindness is a fruit of the Spirit. Kindness is grace and an act of love. It has the power to change lives. We make an impact in the lives of others and ourselves. Kindness spreads love and positivity that inspires others to do the same. Kindness inhabits deep down where we least expect it. When we are open, kindness reveals itself. Kindness is our natural power.

Much of our journey involves learning about power. Learning involves the powers we do not have. We have no power to control ourselves our fate and controlling other people. Many forms of power are illusions. Control may be for a moment. We search for power and if we are sincere, we are quietly awakened. We transform in our vision quests, and we find that kindness is power.

J. Ruth Gendler, a graduate of Stanford University, a kind Jewish writer from Omaha, gives us insight about power. She wrote: "Power made me a coat. For a long time I kept it in the back of my closet. I didn't like to wear it much, but I always took good care of it. When I first started wearing it again, it smelled like mothballs, As I wore it more, it started fitting better, and stopped smelling like mothballs.

"I was afraid if I wore the coat too much, someone would want to take it or else. I would accidentally leave it in the dressing room. It has my name on it, and it really doesn't fit anyone else. When people ask me where I found such a becoming garment, I tell them about the tailor who knows how to make coats that you grow into. You have to find the courage to approach him and ask him to make your coat. Then you must find the patience inside yourself to wear the coat until it fits." (J. Ruth Gendler, *The Book of Qualities*, p. 26)

Need for Kindness of Others

We all need the healing kindness of God. When we see God's loving kindness working through others, we stop and take notice.

It is so sad to live where kindness is not appreciated, but it is considered demeaning. God is kind. Jeremiah 9:24. Kindness is evidence the Holy Spirit lives in us. Kindness is powerful. We are invited to be channels of God's loving kindness to others. Each of us has opportunities to reject the temptations of power.

Spiritual progress is based on developing the fruit of kindness. We must put ourselves in the shoes of others. Kindness means feeling the joys and the pains experienced by others. We examine ourselves to determine if the words we say or write are words we want others to say to us.

By our kindness, others will feel happy to be around us. Their intuition will lead them to also live kind lives. They would feel safe. A surgeon cannot open a brain and discover thoughts that have caused trauma or joy. Thoughts are the foundation of who we think we are. It screws our views of what we think others are.

Kindness brings us closer to God. In your quiet time, reflect on the following words in Proverbs 31:26, Luke 6:35, Galatians 5:22-23, Colossians 3:12, Ephesians 4:32. Kindness is an important fruit of the Spirit. My own writing ministry is designed to inspire and encourage readers on their faith journey.

Kindness is an expression of concern, of care, and consideration of others.

Heartfelt words of encouragement have the power to struggle with pain with the strength of the Lord for us to persevere despite our troubles.

Kindness gives purpose to living. When we incited with kindness, we know why we are traveling on earth to help others. Kindness is the source of our greatest joys. It is the standard for the love of God. It reaches the depths of our souls.

When we are kind, we need inner vision. For each new day is a path for wonder and our lives become visible to God and people we encounter. If we could be mindful of exactly how brief our time is, and how precious each day is.

Kindness When a Spouse Is in the House

Being together all the time is overwhelming. Adjusting to having to share space 24/7 tests kindness. Couples have to be aware of each other's routines. They divide the chores. When my wife Laurel and I retired, we began to experience more than normal togetherness.

Our new retirement home felt like too tight quarters. Even the best couples rub each other the wrong way. We have tried to treat each other as sister and brother in Christ. We decided to forgive each other of anything they do in the future.

Marriage is never easy. We must work at it. Otherwise we would drift into dangerous places. We would end up where we never intended to go. No spouse could love you like Jesus. Read Philippians 2:2-4. God will give us hope for every difficulty. Every relationship has a possibility of a joy relationship.

High expectations or prejudices color and distort relationships. Laurel and I have discovered joy when we least expected it. These healed our souls, opened our hearts, touched us, and changed us in ways we did not expect. They have surprised us. Be open to perceptions.

No day in life belongs to us. Every day is a gift. Destiny travels silently until it arrives. No day is ever the same. Days do not stand still. Each day moves in moments that vanish before our eyes.

Writing is an enlightening metaphor. A writer goes to his or her office desk early each morning to face an empty white page. Memories of the past, both helpful and hurtful, influence what sort of article or book might emerge. Despite her limitations, the work form in its own direction.

The reason we cannot return to where we were years ago is the fact that we all change. Some divide their world into divisions. We realize life in our mother's womb before we are born. We recall our version of childhood to our years of adolescence. Then from old age to death.

One day a farewell from a loved one will be the last one. If any of us are still here, it is the act of divine blessing. Visiting our loved one strengthens human presence.

No human being can understand the full weight of time. We attempt to divide it into sections or divisions. That's how many manage it.

Life is in a constant flow of emergence. When loving kindness is invoked, a window opens in eternal time. Longing for the eternal lights up our imaginations on how we can be kind. Kindness blindness will transform into vision. Any damage will be made whole. Romans 8:28.

When someone is kind to you, the fruit of kindness will surprise us. With serenity and sureness lighting your troubled soul and awakening it for joy.

Hurt is always unfair and unexpected. It poisons the space between us. When we do an intentional act of kindness for those who have injured us, forgiveness cleans things up. Our vision quest is to tap into the deep flow of destiny that is large than our present situations.

After wrestling with writing this book, I received a message of loving kindness. The vision for how to write this book came spontaneously and clearly. The pages in this book have become the pages of my life.

Kindness given and kindness received made for me that deep connection to a God who loves me as I am unconditionally even though I am full of flaws.

Wherever a person loves and cares for us, they have the power of kindness. Don't hesitate to tell those you love, but you feel have hurt you,
that you have decided you do not want to hurt anymore.

Keep loving yourself until you know and are kind to yourself. Self-love means accepting yourself, your beauty, your thoughts, flaws, imperfections, your with and wisdom. Love every part of you. Don't just say kind words. Love yourself until you deeply experience that love.

Kindness and Grace

Kindness is a form of grace. Grace is the permanent atmosphere for divine kindness. Forgiveness and kindness signal the beginning of a new journey of beautiful transformation.

Our lives must be lived forward. Live can be understood backward. Most of the time we continue to be unaware of how blessed we are. Do you have the ability to see? To hear? To understand? To taste? To feel? To smell? On our own we could never have merited the things we take for granted.

We are not aware of the effect we have on each other. This is the place of blessing and loving kindness is so enlivening. Kindness makes us fully alive as powerful and positive intention transform situations and people. Intentional kindness corresponds with our deepest desire of reality for become wholesome.

Kindness is the sincere and voluntary use of resources, talent, and time through acts of love, grace, compassion, generosity, and service. We may be tempted to choice other alternatives.

Kindness includes helpfulness, friendliness, benevolence, courtesy, warmheartedness, thoughtfulness, goodness, sweetness, and love is the center for kindness. Love is the invisible thread that ties kindness to its peers. Love is the origin of empathy is our fractured world. It supports and brings affectionate overtones. Unlike the emotion joy, kindness does not appear as a surprise, but kindness is multiplied with love. Such love is naturally kind.

The Specialness of Kindness

My humble attempt to write this book cannot represent the specialness of kindness. Expressions of the magnificence and magnitude of kindness do not produce a picture of the power of kindness. The most carefully crafted sentences can equal the more substantial, more splendid, and more satisfying aspects of being kind. We are required to branch out beyond the confines of what can be written to immerse ourselves in spiritual strength.

Kindness in God is the act of creation. It preserves our existence. Divine kindness floods into us as a fountain with the powers and blessings of all created kindness. Becoming patient and kind is tough. It is mastered only by the spiritually strong. Patient people ae almost always kind. Love that is truly patient reveals itself in kindness. Kindness sends positive ripples whose impact can only be calculated by God. Kindness has infinite depth. Being kind is a complex action. Kindness is our fundamental nature. Kind people are unconditional and limitless in the ability to include every being, every life form, and every situation that comes within their reach.

Kindness comes to our rescue when we need help. Perfect and lasting kindness is a conscious imitation of God. Our attempts to be like Jesus is the source of sweetness within us, flowing with grace on those within our vision. Kindness makes human capabilities blossom.

Since kindness arises when our mind is free of delusion, being kind is our human genuine essence. Loving kindness can become obscured, buried, and hidden inside of us.

Delusional ways of thinking are conditioned from our day of birth. We can be cut off from kindness, but it is still there. Loving kindness moves us into the wider world. Love is the motivator that inspires us to be mindful, kind, and to continue our spiritual work.

Kindness is our natural state. The acting of kindness allows us to know a deep and profound connection or sense. Sometimes the joy we share of oneness with life. This joy is surprising, miraculous, and supernatural.

The impulse of kindness is an instinct of the most noble parts of us. It is a remnant of the image of God. It is also an attitude of mind Having a genuine intention to live your life as an instrument of God's love, kindness will result.

Authors have written volumes about kindness. These are acts performed spontaneously. The topic of Kindness and the benefits arising from performing kind acts holds both empirical and applied interest. (John Tyler Binet, *The International Journal of Emotional Education*, pp. 49-62.

He wrote, "The self is not something ready-made, but something in continuous formation through choice of action. Even more than honesty, gratitude, or hope, the trait of kindness is identified as one of the top-ranking character strengths valued in society." (John Tyler Binet, *Ibid.*)

There is no substitute for experience.

To understand kindness, we must practice kindness. Intentionally spread kindness. The power of kindness is realized when it is dispersed. Kindness is so memorable, magnetic, and meaningful as we sense that we are incredible, useful, optimistic, and honored to serve others.

Kindness lingers. Kindness picks us up. Dusts us off. Stands tall. It ignites. It heals. It soothes. Kindness involves loving ourselves as we love others.
Loving ourselves as unconditionally as we love those living around us fuels our desire to become our best selves. This also inspires others to be the best version of themselves.

Kindness is so powerful. It can change the world. It changes us as well. It is a bridge to peace and harmony. It erases blame and bitterness. It is a tool that strengthens bonds to God and others.

Kindness is a builder. It is the groundwork for a better future. It taps into the inherent goodness that lives within each of us. It repairs our broken world.

John Killinger included the phrase, "Practice random acts of kindness and senseless acts of beauty" to incite our spiritual awareness. He traced the phrase to Anne Herbert, a writer who lives in the San Francisco area.

In recent decades, people have viewed it on billboards, car bumper stickers, posters, minus, books, bulletins, and periodicals in magazines and newspapers. These words summarize this attitude of spontaneity, love, and joy shared.

Killinger cited Saint Francis, a man who spread kindness wherever he went wit no selfish motives. Francis of Assisi brought us closer to God. Kindness provides us with an experiential clue about how to live in full and complete awareness. (John Killinger, *Raising Your Spiritual Awareness through 365 Simple Gifts from God*, pp. 28-29)

Kindness has power. We can see it even in our wars. A battle between Ukraine and Russia had ended. Earth quivered in the shock. A CBS news correspondent spoke to a gentle Ukrainian woman. She was walking among the wounded giving words of kindness. We are as powerful as we are kind. Kindness is the power of God working in the world. This power makes us divine beings, and not only human beings. We have the power to change the world. Kind acts lighten the world for everybody. They lift our burdens. We become a positive source. Our souls and hearts are filled with unexpected joy.

Do not wait for life to change. Change will come from within. Waiting for things to change is frustrating. Respect this process. Something is happening in your life at this moment. Welcome and honor the changes. The power of kindness is active, mysterious, and magical.

Glimpses of the Power of Kindness

Kindness is an attribute of God. Like a sweet flower on a cold Scottish mountain crag, God speaks in a still, small voice of kindness. Not to be kind is not to be like Christ.

Jesus' sacrifice produced the foundation for human salvation. Jesus died as a kindness for humanity. God the Father indulged in kindness. Like his father, Jesus did the same. So we have an obligation to reciprocate and appreciate Jesus' acts of kindness. Jesus was the messenger of God on earth.

We are to accept God's kindness in a proper manner. John Wesley wrote, "Doth not kindness melt you." (John Wesley, *A Collection of Hymns for the People Called Methodists*, p. 226) Wesley also noted that we are to love God's kindness.

Golden threads must be woven into life texture. Nothing less than the kindness of Christ is accepted as the pattern with which we create character. Progress is made each day. The lesson has not been learned if we continue to be rude, unkind, uncontrolled anger, sharp in speech, We have to attend God's school of life to attain the kindness fruit.

Kindness gave Christianity a unique approach to achieve conversion to Christ of non-believers. Preaching to convert non-Christians saved the souls of non-Christians. Non-believers were promised abundant gifts from God's loving kindness.

We accomplish this by compelling every thought, word, and deed into one channel until kindness is a permanent part of our lives. It is unconditional and boundless. A gentle rain waters all the plants skipping none.

Those rains of kindness have no stopping point. We turn our kindness to appreciation of others. We adore and celebrate every deed of kindness. We give them our rapt attention, befriend them, look for the good in them, and offer no hostility. Our kindness is turned outwards to our friends, family, strangers, enemies, and all people.

We see we love all life forms from trees to flowers, lakes, and rivers, rocks and soil. We have the enlightened insight that everything exists for our good. The universe is here to support and serve us in our ability to live with eternal joy. When we are one with all life, the joys of others becomes yours as well. The service and kindness we offer brings them joy, which expands our joy as well. Why limit this awesome joy? Matthew 5:44.

God's grace and love have eternal depth. These fruits are our transformed nature. Philippians 2:13. When we shop for apples, we go to Nebraska City to the huge apple orchard. We find it easier to pick apples from the lower branches. As we tune into kindness, we cultivate this biblical fruit four easily love people. Others, even our worst enemies represent apples growing in the top of the tree.

As we get comfortable giving our apples of love to our family, loved ones, and then friends, we eventually give them to those with whom we have differences and difficulties.

When we are ready and willing to embrace our worst enemies with kindness joyfully and wholeheartedly. Until then, don't force it. Start with the low-hanging fruit.

Kind deeds are the sensitivity toward the mental, physical, and emotional needs with a willingness to meet those needs. Jesus demonstrated his power in the physical realm. Jesus had power to heal in the spiritual realm as well.

"Are you the coming one?" asked friends of John the Baptist. Luke 7:20. Jesus did not give a simple answer. Jesus said to tell John the things they had seen him do. Luke 7:22.

Kindness is a powerful witness to the world. It is the establishment that works in obvious but unconscious ways. The church, as a redemptive presence, helps shape the world.

We witness kindness everywhere. Nebraska and the whole Midwest has endured ice and snow. From the window of our home office, my wife and I experienced seeing a flower rising up through the snow. The snow was its white blanket.

We have often felt alone with Laurel's fight with cancer. We too often forget as your presence is under the snow of pain. Beneath the snow is solid ground.

It would be impossible to calculate the exact impact the church makes.
The church is not of the spirit of the world. That power is the power of the evil ones. John 15:19. Jesus then compared the relationship of the church toward the world with his own relationship to the world. John 17:14.

All that is in the world such as lust of the flesh, the pride of life is not of the Father. I John 2:15-16. The power of the Holy Spirit belongs to the whole body and not just a part. We are not to invalidate her witness through the fruit of kindness that speaks to the powers of the world.

The resurrection of Jesus changes everything. We no longer have to fear death. Let us know the victory in every way. May all cancer cells burst forth with everlasting life.

The power of loving kindness will strengthen all who suffer from cancer. This awful hardship can draw us closer in our gatherings in home, hospital, and church.

New life can ooze out of the church of kindness. We can look to the future with hope that we cannot yet fathom. One day we will know the full revelation of Christ. Romans 1:8-10.

The apostle Paul wrote those words to the Roman Christians. They were encouraged to carry on their faith, hope, and loving kindness. The words also encourage people who are afflicted with cancer and all forms of disease. Isaiah 40:30-31.

The Difference in Kindness

Love and kindness are never wasted. Loving kindness makes a difference. Being kind blesses the one who receives and mostly it rewards the one who gives. Kindness consists of loving people more than they deserve.

We cannot be kind too soon. We never know how soon it will be too late. Learn the art of joyful loving kindness. The Holy Spirit knows where we need to be and understands where we really desire to go. God has given us a clear map.

Losses pile up as we continue to live. People we love disappear. We lose money, careers, and at times we think we know so few people now. We lose our dreams.

There are few things we can control. We have the power to feel, to choose, to think. We are able to take responsibility for ourselves and for our lives. We learn to see beyond our fears. We need to find freedom.

A part of us still feels frozen, powerless, and abandoned when we face certain situations. Watch where you were when you were but a child. Be kind to that child. Forgive them for being afraid. The reasons are valid. And they are reasonable. Those reasons come from a long time ago. This is now. Give yourself a break. See the kindness in a stranger's smile. Feel the tenderness, affection, and respect.

Go out and embrace your kindness connection. Embrace the unexpected joys. Stay open. Keep on loving yourself. Observe how much better and how much kinder life is. You will see more, feel more, and be more than you have ever been before.

You are more sensitive to energies, places, things, and people. You will also become sensitive to any resolved issues inside of yourself in all those whom you will encounter.

This will bring you joy. The extraordinary power of kindness emerge gently. Be who you really are in your loving kindness. When you look back and honestly view your past, look tenderly at all the events both good and bad. Examine the past wit the eyes of your soul. Your soul teaches you. Permit yourself to have all your experiences. All these adventures were necessary. Select the treasures from each. It is your price for living. Take one step at a time. Let your faithfulness be strong.

One power we gain on our journey is the ability to redefine what we believe. We see things in a new way. Watch yourself. You can change yourself, but you cannot change others. Watch what you think. Watch what you say. Watch how you feel. Watch how you act. Watch how you react.

Every single human being has their personal issues. And humans can and do forgive. Now is the time to practice the fruit of kindness understanding, and forgiveness for ourselves. Kindness is a gift from the Holy Spirit. The spirit is your inner voice. Listen to the whispers of your soul. Now is the time of miracles and magic. Our future is not limited to our past. God knows that eternal truth. The Spirit will teach you. You will see things as you have never seen.

When all of our powers are stripped away, we can still practice the power of self-love. No one can take way that power. Self-love will make any situation better. We will understand events and people on a much deeper way than we have ever experienced.

We will find power in kindness along with grace, love, comfort, faith, and joy. Tell yourself how well you are doing. You may discover more than you thought.

Take a break. Change your perspective.

Chapter Two

The Biblical View of Kindness

The Bible has a lot to say about kindness. Our Scriptures offer a perfect model in Jesus. The Bible teaches that kindness, a fruit of the Holy Spirit, takes time to grow in us. Reading the Bible is maintaining discipline to do it consistently. To read and to pray early each morning makes a difference in my energy level. My simple spiritual practices involve simple spiritual disciplines.

It's never easy to be kind. Many people find it difficult to be kind. I John 4:8 tells us God is love. In God's love we know that God is kind. We would be more like God if we practiced kindness. Matthew 5:43-48. Jesus' words in this passage were recorded in the Greek language. His original words were spoken in Aramaic. The ideal life would be to become like Christ Jesus. What would our homes and churches be like if all the members "die to self," and let kindness be their goal? Being kind affects our witness.

The biblical record has multitudes of examples of kindness. Ephesians 4:32, I Thessalonians 2:7, Romans 15:1, I Timothy 2:24-25. We must show kindness to every person we encounter who are weak in the faith. Being kind means using words gently. Proverbs 15:1-5, 25:11-15, Matthew 5:16.

Jesus assured us that the kindness we show to others has its rewards. Kindness begets kindness. Jesus told us to do to others the good we would like them to do for us. Giving cups of cold water as welcome gifts is at the heart of kindness. Matthew 10:40-42. This biblical statement makes a powerful claim about the identification of believers with Jesus and also with God.

Kindness in the biblical Jewish culture was significant. Extending kindness to others was important. Matthew 18:5, Hebrews 13:2.

We see Jesus in people that we encounter. We are to be kind to anyone in need. Such kindness carries its own reward from God. Kindness is rooted in the life of Jesus.

The grace of God has been bestowed on us. So we do acts of kindness as we pray to be a little kinder and to a little blinder to the faults of those around us.

The Radical Call of Kindness

Kindness is a radical call. It is not that we have courage at our last days on earth. Kindness in life is the joy of the Lord showing through in all of our living years on this earth.

Kind people are not quickly forgotten. The stories we hear after they are gone are about their spirit of kindness. Their kindnesses run deep and wide. Most of us are now finding out that kindness is quite uncommon. Kindness has become a forgotten characteristic. To become a Christ-like follower, kindness must shape and define us. We do not understand the power of kindness. My ministry of writing includes the rediscovery of kindness.

I wrote this book out of frustration that those who represent the gospel are caustic and hostile. Unkindness gets us nowhere in sharing the gospel. Kindness is not incompatible with courage. Kindness is courage. Kindness is fierce, not to be mistaken for just being nice.

Kindness is found throughout the Bible. Niceness is not found in scripture.
Disciples of Christ walk the dangerous and risky road of kindness. Kindness is the biblical way for living. It is a fruit of

the Spirit in Saint Paul's short list in Galatians 5. It is the result of the Holy Spirit acting in our lives.

Kindness has the power to change lives. Repentance changes lives. Kindness leads us to doing it. Kindness helps us negotiate in a time when few negotiate. Kindness is the higher ground that reveals the middle ground and the common ground. Psalm 141:5.

Kindness is a difficult adventure. Micah 6:8 urges us to love kindness. The Bible uses the term loving kindness to insure no separation between kindness and love. The Bible points us to extraordinary kindness that has the potential to become contagious.

Kindness is a dimension of the grace of God. Biblical kindness, as Jesus lived it is a presentation of he highest hope for our renewal needed now, in this moment.

Kindness embodies grace, love, and truth lived out in our relationships with others.

God is kind. Psalm 86:5. The kindness of God prompted redemption. That kindness draws us toward God. Romans 2:4, Titus 3:4. As "imitators of God," we must be kind. Ephesians 5:1.

Our kind actions must come from pure and sincere motives. Romans 12:9. From a biblical perspective, we must demonstrate kindness with poise, not always getting our way. Kindness results in understanding and sympathy. I Peter 3:8. Kindness causes us to be patient, long suffering, and tolerant. I Thessalonians 6:18.

The Bible tells us to be kind. That's straightforward. Being kind is not something we just get out of bed in the morning, and we are kind. We might say, "Beginning today, I will be a kind person." The best intensions will fail if we depend on our own strength.

Paul called kindness a fruit of the Spirit, because it cannot become effective without the Holy Spirit continuing to work in our lives. John 15:5.

As we live in the Spirit, the command to be kind echoes through each day in our lives. Ephesians :31-32. The Bible points out to us that kindness produces positive results. Proverbs 11:17.

Kindness opens doors for ministry and service. Barnabas was called the son of encouragement. He sold a field and gave the money for relief of the saints. Acts 4:37. He was sensitive to hurting people. Kindness softens the difficult hearts of humanity. Proverbs 15:1. No influence is so powerful as our practice of kindness. It makes a difference.

In our cultivation of the fruit of kindness, we discover inexhaustible resources of the dynamic Holy Spirit, whom God has graciously poured out on us. Zechariah 4:6. Knowing God is to know the Word we live by.

We meet life on the level of daily experience. Experiencing life is our constant companion.

Biblical kindness is speaking kind words to others. Proverbs 12:25. The Bible tells us God has given promises to those who are kind. Proverbs 11:17, 19:17, Hebrews 6:10 indicates that God rewards those who are kind.

Kindness is embodied in Jesus. John 1:1, 14. He calls us to hear him and live by his Word. When this Word is truly heard, the response comes from deep down in our inner souls.

God's character gives loving kindness towards us. Without the kindness of God, we would be lost. Scripture reveals that we need to make a commitment to be kind to others as God has been kind to us. God's kindness is undeserved and unearned. God's kindness motivates us to be kind to others. Ephesians 4:32.

Kindness is expressed in the context of a relationship. Loving kindness is evident in marriage. Genesis 20:13. Fathers and sons are kind. Genesis 47:29, Ruth 1:8. The host and a guest express kindness. Genesis 19:19. Friends are kind to each other. I Samuel 20:8, II Samuel 16:17, Job 6:14, Proverbs 20:18.

Abimelech urges Abraham to respond to the kindness he has been shown, by showing kindness in return. Genesis 21:23. Abimelech received Abraham as a guest. Genesis 20:15. He gave him kind hospitality and he expects hospitality in return, both to him and the country where Abraham is a sojourner.

An orthodox summary of the attributes of God and the high place given to loving kindness. Exodus 34:6. Kindness is a characteristic of God rather than human beings. It is rooted in the divine nature.

The kindness relationship requires mutually beneficial action, but a right will and attitude. Loving kindness is the expression of faithfulness and loyalty. The interpretation of his biblical truth is that when God entered into a covenant with Israel, God was bound for showing kindness to them. God's kindness is unfailing and enduring. (Robin Routledge, "Hesed as Obligation: A Re-examination," Tyndale Bulletin, 46, pp. 55-80, 1995)

God's kindness and grace go together in the Bible. Biblical faith implies a willingness to live as a kind human being. Romans 8:24-25. As Christians, we do not happen to believe and obey the gospel because of rational arguments or mountaintop experiences.

Kindness for the Undeserving

God helps the undeserving. Scripture informs that kindness depends solely on God in the form of grace. Psalm 51:1. The Psalmist recognizes that sin has distorted his relationship with God. The kindness shows God's continuing faithfulness and love toward the children. There is a divine commitment to the relationship that assures loyalty in accordance with it.

God's loving kindness graciously seeks the continuing acceptance of people's failures and continues the relationship in light of all that threatens it. God loves us more than we can imagine. Love is a choice. When love comes, we expect to know it by our evoked feelings.

Kindness is a loving commitment within the context of a relationship. It includes both our faithfulness and our loyalty. Loving kindness is mutual ways to reciprocate. Kindness is viewed as a mutual obligation in our faithfulness, obedience, and devotion. It is at the heart of maintaining fellowship with the divine lover. God promises forgiveness and restoration based on a new covenant, proven by renewed kindness within the restored community. Psalm 98:2-3.

Biblical kindness brings the shiny face of God to warm us. Numbers 6:24-26. This biblical assurance says that we all feel the power and radiance contained in this touching blessing.

These scriptural images comfort, protect, heal, and bless us. Imagine the radiant face of God looking directly at your face with loving kindness. Fell the shining warmth filling your entire body.

Being a child in the arms of God gives us a sense of littleness and helplessness. Hosea 11:3-4 gives us images of being held close, receiving food, or holding on to a parent or a spouse as we learn to walk.

Past, future, and present, God is the father who picks us up and snuggles us to the cheek with a loving warmness. We know tat we are now wrapped in love.

I have now lived long enough to understand that other people bring us the best in life or distress and panful experiences. Biblical loving kindness helps us to realize the power each of us has with each other to build up or break down. I Thessalonians 5:11.

Each day is enriched when we realize that our lives are finite. Seize the day. All we ever have is the present moment. The only place where w find God is in the now. Each moment is important. Psalm 90:12.

God is both father and mother to us. We are invited to reach out to God. The biblical image is of God, bonded to us, hearing our distress and reaching out to hold us close, always looking for ways to make it better. Knowing this is the promised response of God, we remind ourselves to reach out to God and ask for help when life hurts. Isaiah 66:13.

We often fail to see that we do have choices we ca make when we become uncomfortable. We could focus on how terrible we feel. We can imagine how huge our problems are. We can lament about nobody understanding us. There is no clear road map for dealing with the sad things of life. Matthew 7:7.

Scripture reveals that life unexpectedly asks of us something we believe is so enormous and overwhelming that we don't think we could handle it. We want to be relieved of the pain and exonerated from all that has passed. We feel helpless and vulnerable. That is the now moment to throw ourselves into the loving kindness and mercy of God.

The Bible anguishes that every person has troubles. All of us have sinned and lost the glory of God. At times we invite troubles by choices we make. No life is without troubles.

God will help us to change our perspective. Instead of expressing our difficulties in a negative way, we can look at them with new eyes.

Sharpen the way that we look at our struggles so that we can actually see the gift that is hidden in them. Psalm 34:17.

We worry and become anxious and stuck as we focus on the "what ifs" of our lives or those "if onlys" that are dragged along with them. Why focus on things we can't control? God knows all about us. God does not think like we do. The ways of God are not our ways.

Let the joy of the Lord be your strength. Philippians 4:6.

Chapter Three

The Evangelism of Kindness

Kindness needs faithful practice every day. Acts of kindness are often on-the-spot, in the moment, and a surprise. Specific acts of kindness do not come when we feel like it. Kindness requires a seeking out. We are looking to enable the needs of others. Kindness is the new evangelism.

The concept of kindness is simple, but that does not mean it is effortless. We do not know how to be kind. My critics say that that is absurd. I intend to walk you through the who, what, when, where, and how in writing this book.

People say things on social media, email, and texts that they would not utter our loud or face to face. Kindness is easily quashed unless we are purposeful about showing it. Kindness simply isn't the priority in this moment in time. Unhappy wives are told, "You don't have to take that from him." Husbands are told, "Show her who is the boss."

In the past few decades, we have been essentially told to become cold, to back off, to withdraw because you deserve better. We shut off feelings entirely. We just suck it up. Kindness takes effort.

Living in an unkind world is highly dissatisfying. We all want to come home to a kind home. Our children want to ride home in the school bus to meet a kind mother and father. Nobody wants to work in a hostile workplace. We want our colleagues to respect us.

Kindness is the outward face of unconditional love. We are certainly imperfect, but we love being married to someone who works at marriage. Only then will our children have a mom and dad who are committed to each other for life.

Kindness Evangelism

Kindness is a simple tool that brings dramatic results for restoring, building, and improving any relationship. Imagine yourself being irritated with their spouse, boss, parent or child. We keep on telling others about our personal irritation and we become even more irritated.

Kindness works better than our words. Set out to be kind to them and about them. Find something positive or praiseworthy about that person. You will become less irritated. If we continue to be negative, does it really change anything in the end? Be gracious in the face of harshness. Practicing kindness causes us to be kind.

To be kind requires that we say nothing negative about our loved one. Say nothing hurtful to them or anybody else. Each day find one positive thing that you can sincerely affirm or praise about that person. Tell them. And tell others. Your kindness will build something powerful, beautiful, and transformative. As we practice evangelism, we are doing kindness and obeying the Great Commission.

Kindness evangelism was highlighted for me during 20 years of the NCAA College World Series in Omaha, Nebraska. Churches throughout Nebraska used kindness to reach the thousands of people who attend the baseball championship. They support a baseball clinic for youth led by major league stars. They hold a dinner just before the series begins. And we bought thousands of bottles of cold water to offer an act of kindness as the weather is always hot in Omaha in June. We gave kindness to thirsty people, free of charge, and no strings attached. During that week, the medium became the message.

During my 70 years of ministry, I have attempted many kinds of evangelism strategies. Crusade evangelism, vision quests in churches, schools, prisons, and preaching evangelism.

When our efforts are blessed by God, each attempt can be effective in reaching unchurched people. Ice cold water on a sizzling hot day was so refreshing. Most just uttered a quick thank you. Some talked to us, asking who we were and why we were doing this kindness.

Giving water offered a chance to offer a witness to God's loving kindness outside a church building. Most of the visiting crowd were evangelicals such as Baptists, Methodists, and other groups. The College World Series is called the Southeastern Conference Invitational as half of the teams traveled to Omaha. South Carolina, Louisiana State, Vanderbilt, Mississippi, and Mississippi State are recent winners. They offered words of thanks and appreciation for the ministry. Some even asked for prayer. A few discussed their need for a living faith.

All of the givers of refreshing cold water agreed that kindness is a powerful witness, a deeper refreshment than the cold water as a symbol of Christ's love.

Other acts of kindness that any person or church can do includes lawn care, snow removal, free coffee at highway rest areas, oil changes, umbrella escorts on rainy days. Acts of kindness are appreciated by seniors, single mothers, the poor, the sick, and those needing a care center or nursing homes. Possibilities are endless.

Kindness evangelism is doing small things for needy people in the name of Jesus. Little acts bring big results. Kindness is the language which the deaf or dumb can speak and understand.

Free ministries such as the gift of cold water at a major sports event offers a picture of the grace of God. Kindness evangelism is a precious gift that can never be repaid. It is servant evangelism with deeps of love, words of love, and the gifts of time.

God's love must be communicated person to person. Deeds of love allow us to touch the souls of those we serve. Deeds of kindness brings attention and questions from seekers of a joy-filled life. There is no sales' pitch needed. Kindness is not a one-shot event. Sharing Jesus with our neighbors is the key rather than a project.

Kindness is "high grace." It is loving and accepting people. If Jesus enjoyed watching the college world series, he would be among those giving cold water to thirsty people who need his love.

People were created in the image of God. Kindness leads us to do things that are not expected or even necessary. When people are changed, the world will be changed. The scope of the task to change the world feels overwhelming.

Kindness evangelism does not get a huge emphasis in the Hebrew Bible or the Old Testament. It's not like some modern evangelism strategies.

Jesus is the perfect example of this fruit of the Spirit. During his three years of ministry, he looked toward the needs of others. Jesus was always one to be counted on. Jesus shared the Good News with kindness.

We miss doing deeds of kindness as we think we are too busy. We must slow down and open our eyes. We are required to show kindness to everyone. Being an evangelistic church required taking time for others. Kindness brings the essence of evangelism. Kindness is our drinking of living water to unbelievers.

Kindness is a powerful tool for reaching people. Kindness draws unbelievers toward Christ Jesus. Kind deeds will open the door. Many Christians have struggled to do evangelism.

Simple acts of kindness can transform the culture of meanness. There is no shortage of people being nasty. Kindness evangelism faces the cruelty all around us. Kindness is simple but challenging. It is global. It is contagious.

Most believers have thought of evangelism as the invitation for those outside the church to experience the love and grace by joining us inside of a church. What if simple acts of kindness to hose beyond the walls of our churches became an effective way to do evangelism?

The Holy Spirit will attune our spiritual ears to God's voice. Basic kindness is powerful. During the 23 years as campus minister for Southeast Community College in Lincoln, students came up with a distinct outreach plan. Instead of having the traditional able lined up next to all the church groups, they decided to offer random acts of kindness to students roaring the campus between classes.

Kindness evangelism allows the presence of Christ to shine as we live. Anybody who encounters us will find the loving kindness of God. Fan the flames of kindness for everybody who crosses your pathway.

Kindness is simple but challenging. The reactions create many opportunities for our student leaders to begin conversations. We discovered that kindness attracted positive attention to our ministry. We stood out from the crowd within the community on the campus.

Kindness can become a form of effective evangelism anywhere beyond the churches that brings a deeper connection. Kindness is central to our mission and values. It will create a distinct culture for any ministry.

I have experienced just about every evangelism method of evangelism. Virtually any method can be used by God to enable people to discover faith in Christ. No one biblical method can communicate the timeless truths of the gospel. We are dealing with people who are journeying through life with various degrees of awareness about God and spiritual life.

Evangelism should respect the integrity of other journeys. Evangelism challenges people to do further on their journeys. Timing is everything in influencing the course of a journey. We must be sensitive to when and how we share.

Kindness evangelism does not understand conversion as the end of a process. It is the beginning of a discipleship process to experience their special guidance to the way of Christ, a way of loving kindness.

A Spirit of Joy congregation accepts a higher level of responsibility, as it commits to be flexible and open in nurturing the journey process. With the fruit of the spirit including kindness, the church encourages discerning the corporate journey of the congregation and in the individual journeys of its members and friends of the church and non-believers living in the church's community.

As relationships with all these groups begin and blossom, we find partners who may link to our own journeys. We have previously written a chapter on preaching as a significant way the articulation concerning the journey.

Preaching involves the preparation and delivery of biblical messages that clarify, foster, and encourage the spiritual journeys. Jesus does that in his sermon on the mount. Matthew 5-7.

Preaching requires that the decision of what texts to use be chosen with the demands and needs of the special spiritual journeys of those who hear the sermons. Hebrews 13:7. Preaching about issue we have no personal experience of produces shallow advice and leads people into journey difficulties.

Chapter Four

The Church of Kindness

We do not learn kindness by ourselves alone. To have a kind heart, we must be filled with the fruit of the Holy Spirit. The church shares training and discipline. The Holy Spirit will enable us to learn this lesson.

Humans are social beings. We live in community with each other. Organizations such as church congregations acknowledge innate interdependence and accepting responsibility.

Congregations that want to respond to the call of God but don't know how to reach the destination of God for them.

Joining Together for Personal Fulfillment

God calls individuals to join together to go on their own spiritual journeys. The group exists for the benefit of its individual members. The Bible does not give many stories about small groups, except for the stories of the journeys of Jesus and his twelve disciples. Matthew 10:5-8.

We do not much about how God prepared those original disciples for their group spiritual journey. It was not a long time before the followers of Jesus from an crease to a few dozen to multiplied thousands throughout the Roman Empire. Congregations founded and organized by the disciples were different. The new gatherings were not closed or temporary groups. Acts 2:42-47, 4:32-37.

A local church, as a body of believers, has an identity that goes beyond the individuals who make up the fellowship. Churches take on a differing look, based on their cultural setting.

The seven churches in Revelation are addressed as if each one were an individual that was responsible for its own spiritual journey. Some of these early congregations were not faithful in their spiritual journey. Others were more faithful.

Just because some congregations were described as unfaithful, there were individuals within them had rejected God's call. Revelation 2:24 tells us there were a faithful few in the Thyatira church who were not failing in their spiritual journey.

In the New Testament, there are some descriptions of congregational spiritual journeys. The apostle Paul and others wrote letters addressed to specific churches to the issues within the churches. Their spiritual journeys were linked together, but there was lack of cooperation between individuals.

Acts gives a historical account of the early church. Acts give no records on the journeys of special churches. It tells a lot about Paul and Peter, and the empowerment of some certain members to provided needed segments.
Acts 6:1-6.

Antioch is one of the churches mentioned as the concern for a love offering collection. Acts 11:27-30. It describes the ordination of Paul and Barnabas for their first missionary journey. Acts 13:1-3.

Congregational spiritual journeys are more complex than individual spiritual journeys. The group journey is the collection expression of a number of individual journeys.

Paul used two metaphors. One was the body of Christ, composed of many differing but equal members. I Corinthians 12. The other is a building composed of bricks. When the bricks are placed together, they create a house of God. Ephesians 2.

My sense of calling in the journey impacts the spiritual journeys of other people, as well as the collection journey of the church to which I belong. No individual journey is acted out in isolation. Individual calls to ministry impacts the ministry of the church. The life of each individual parish becomes the visible celebration of the interplay between individual spiritual journeys.

The church has served as a source of grace and wisdom. It is a place of sharing sacred soul stories of our God experiences and the ways that we are called to mirror the mystery as we find joy of the fruit that is now housed within us. In this mirroring, we can move and dance in delight.

Some have lost sight of the purpose of the church. A church can use statements of purpose, mission, and vision. Some think the purpose of a church is to fill as many pews as possible. Some declare that it's purpose is to keep clergy employed. The purpose of the church is to join God in loving kindness and joy.

The inverse of taking life for granted is to become mindful of small kindnesses. Life need not be habitual. The church of kindness knows that it is a miracle just to be alive.

During my ministry of bringing joy to the world with my writing and preaching, I have used my gifts as an artist. I have often been discouraged in making my vision quest. Like many older men, I fall asleep, and God sends power to produce an oil painting or a book.

When we toil and work in service to Christ, kindness results. Christ himself comes and puts on our canvas the touches of beauty which our own hands cannot produce.

The strength of Christian faith depends on healthy, spiritually nourishing congregations. Congregations are the cradle of the juices of joy. Congregations are in a constant place for change. Flourishing congregations successfully deal with the emotions and reality of change. Members come and go, pastoral leadership, lay leadership, needs of the community shift.

A church in a toxic environment will have a high staff turnover, unusual secret keeping, or a major membership rift or exodus. Member squabble over power. Abusers are protected while victims are ignored. We cannot assume that most churches are heathy. Congregations change into authoritarian places.

There is no magic bullet for restoring a church into a Church of Kindness or a Spirit of Joy Church. Things get uglier before they become better. Complaining and fighting are tactics used. The doors are guarded by gatekeepers who attempt to identify people seeking to join in membership by labels, categories, or cultural religious beliefs. A toxic church is spiritual poison. Toxic congregations are filled with cliques. Small groups of friends exclude others or refuse to give others a chance to be in the circle.

A golden rule for church conflict is to always talk with the person involved directly. Toxic churches spread unhealthy gossip. It is like pouring gasoline on a fire.

God calls lay and clergy to imperfect congregations where we are expected to use our graces, gifts, and talents to enable a church to get closer to what God wants.

Like some of my oil paintings, they look good from a distance. A closer look at my artwork reveals brush strokes, little messes everywhere. Until we get to heaven, every single congregation will have imperfect brush strokes. (James E. McReynolds, *Spirit of Joy Church*, pp. 30-39)

The Church of Joy contains element all pastors would love to have. This joy is brought about as a Church of Kindness. These rare congregations seek to cultivate a buoyant, joyous sense of kindness of God in our daily lives, Alexander Maclaren said. The fate of our churches is their primary concern. Tied to that concern is the fate of the earth. This earth is suffering from the weight of us who live there.

Joy and kindness should be passed on. Any congregation that harbors guilt and shame, lacks grace and forgiveness is extremely rigid, authoritarian, ruled by black and white rules of doctrines, will ultimately become disoriented when life does not meet their expected outcomes.

Freedom from guilt and shame comes as we accept and share the grace of God. God is honored when we do our best to make things right with God, others, and ourselves. Only then are we free to move forward in a positive and graceful way.

The church of kindness is not one filled with gossip or backbiting. It is not ruled by deacons and elders or some abusive pastor. The fruit of the Spirit is exchanged for works of the flesh.

Members of any church should not exhibit meanness. Those unkind people find a foothold in the church fellowship. Some may be kind to one another, but there is no grace and love.

Kindness is a manner of being shaped by love. he congregation responds to conflicts wit empathy. We cannot separate kindness from love. Being nice to those we agree with is not how love works. This covers the indifference that is lovelessness.

Kindness and love are tied together. Loveless people are not willing to put in the work of being kind. They are not willing to rock the boat when they clearly see it sinking.

Unfortunately most churches are not known for kindness. The power up and attack when they feel marginalized or on the defense. Their reflex is to fight those in opposition. They lead with a caustic harshness, and they do tremendous damage to the gospel witness.

Made in God's image, we are called to stir up our spiritual sisters and brothers to love with kind deeds. Love demands that we in the church go on to perfection. Love forgives all infirmities.

All believers face life challenges. Our journey through these trying times brings losses and fears. Kind people lose jobs, but they are able to move on in a different direction. The community of kindness adapts to changing circumstances without losing the desire to fulfill our calling from God.

Numbness and shock will be our early response. Strong oak trees fight the winds and break. A willow tree bends and survives.

He church of kindness sends encouraging notes just when they are needed. The make phone calls just to ask how we have been doing after an illness. The pastor will come when called for any time of day or night. These acts of kindness are ways that God uses to communicate loving kindness.

Healing kindness helps us to be strong. It's easier to be courageous when you are not alone. The First Church of Kindness of any denomination is founded on the times when Divine presence is felt. God is always at work bringing the fruit of kindness to ripeness.

Churches have a negative bias as they reach connection. Kind churches marvel at the positive impact. People who do kind deeds consistently underestimate how much it was appreciated. Every one of us has the capacity to be kind and to change the world. A gentle, tender heart houses a sympatric spirit that feels the pain and suffering of others. God will use us to pour blessings on everybody we encounter on our path through life. Our reward is to be able to share in the blessing.

When kindness penetrates our souls, we are calm and joyous. Loving like an awakened being. Loving kindness allows grace and love to flourish. Being kind fills our lives with times of joy. Kindness brings unintentional awareness of our thoughts, feelings, and experiences just as they are. We will discover our shared, imperfect humanness that will create self-love and compassion. We can adore and love kindness as the entry point to self-love.

The Adoring Love of Kindness

Kindness is love that is intimate with goodness. Kind people value and cherish joy. They find worth in every human being. Kindness impacts our world.

Kindness embraces suffering. Kindness recognizes our shared ability to suffer. It responds by seeking to alleviate that suffering. The joys of kindness are intimate with joyful appreciation and celebration.

Kindness is the choice of the willing heart. Genuine kindness results from God's mercy to us. Powerful kindness requires a surrendered heart. The Apostle Paul calls the Ephesian church to higher ground. Kindness is the higher ground. Ephesians 4:1-6.

Paul pleads for them to take the high road. Paul defines what "walking worthy" looks like. Paul is writing the letter from prison.

The Church of Kindness is in unity. They believe there is one body, one spirit, one hope, and one lord. There is one faith, one baptism, and one God and Father.

Every believer has the gift of grace. Ephesians 4:7-16. Paul gives us specific requirements for a kind and tender heart. Ephesians 4:25-32. Acts of kindness will be remembered as they opens souls even better than miracles. Believers are still searching for a church that teaches a kind life rather than a rigid system of beliefs. Matthew 13:45-46. This a hopeful vision quest for Christianity.

In our fast paced, impatient, and overly stimulated world, kindness stands out. The congregation is committed to underwriting the sending, caring and reaching out to others. Kindness is seen, heard, and felt by the world.

Kindness makes us relationship whisperers. God uses kindness in a mysterious way. Kindness will empower us to change some things that we able to change. We can change our attitude, our actions, and reactions. We are summoned to give dignity to others.

Kindness revolutionizes relationships. It is truly a superpower. It is the essence of who we are in Christ. We see the glory of God reflected in Jesus. The Church of Kindness partners with the Spirit for us to be transformed so reflect kindness to others.

They will see the fruit in our living and understand how loving God is. Jesus used the image of a kind Father who is eager to forgive. The mother hen is another image that Jesus used. The hen gathers her chicks.

Jesus used other things such as God as our friend, a vineyard keeper, light, living water, and wine. Jesus said, "Whoever sees me sees the Father." Colossians 1:15, 19-20. Jesus alluded to his unique relationship with the Father. Matthew 11:17. The possibilities of heaven intrigues even unbelievers.

The Sunday after the Twin Towers disaster in New York, my church in Weeping Water was filled. People began praying. The church overflowed for several weeks. Church members did not want to be isolated. Members knew that any of us could die in the blink of an eye. This truth brought about reflections on the miserable condition of the earth because of our failure to love one another and offer kindness.

Terrorists plan new nuclear threats every day. Most powerful nations hold on to stockpiles. We now have the power to destroy the whole planet earth. God wants us to remain calm in the midst of the darkness and stormy surroundings. Remain serene. With God all things are possible. Return evil unkindness into kindness.

The Church of Kindness will not demonize its enemies. When they attempt to demonize the church, pray for them. Attempt to do God's will as we return good for evil.

Living in peace is the gift God wants to give. The Spirit of Joy Church has decided to give up resentment and decide to forgive. They give up hatred and return kindness and goodness for evil. They don't complain, but they decide to be grateful. They give up sadness and take on hopefulness. The give up anger and choose to be patient.
This kind of thinking helps control our thoughts and actions. When we are sick, we follow our physician's orders. We drink lots of water. We get plenty of sleep. We take the pills. We do the suggested exercises. We must have the grace to say, "Thy will be done."

Faith gives us the confidence to trust God in all circumstances. As my dear wife is recovering from breast cancer, faithful medical people told us, " This is not your fault. Cancer is limited. Cancer cannot cripple love. It can't shatter hope. It cannot destroy peace. It cannot destroy a friendship or a marriage."

We faithful Christians know that cancer cannot shut out our joyful moments. It can enter our bodies but not our souls. Our strength is in Jesus. Never let self-pity make you sad and miserable. We not placed on this earth by chance.

God knows all about us. Our smiles are possible when we are sorrowful and in pain. Smiles show that the Holy Spirit is living in us.

God created us to be joyful. God wants us to enjoy kindness with love and grace oozing with joy and kindness in the next world, and in this one as well.

We play a role in each other's lives. Each one has a journey. We pray traveling mercies with the power to unleash some good, acceptance, and awareness. May we be a force for good to ourselves, our families, and our church.

Too many churches have a capacity to show unkindness. They rush to create power and to exercise strength and power over other people. They had the option to be kind, but they choose to be hurtful. That door leads to nowhere.

God broods over us with unconditional love. God calls us with a deep love. Restless souls find their rest in God. God has promised not to lead us as orphans through the circumstances of our lives.

The Bible gives us the name Emmanuel which means "God with us." Matthew 1:23 quoting Isaiah 7:14. The psalmist wrote of the abiding presence of God in Psalm 139:1-18.

The Garden of Kind Souls

Kind souls are like a garden. Kind thoughts are the roots. Kind deeds are the fruits. Kind words are the blossoms. No wisdom is greater than expressions of kindness. The more you nurture and water kindness, the calmer and happier you will become.

The church with a Spirit of Joy will expand loving kindness. This church can do nothing but spread it in all directions. Imagine what expanding and touching. Go to people you know, people you don't know, people you have difficulty with, and the people you love. Whoever is touched by your kindness will be changed.

Imagine a loved one in front of you. Begin to wish them well. Even if they have made bad choices, ask God to protect them from danger. Pray that they are healthy and strong. Let the kindness come from you. Say whatever is meaningful to you. Don't think that speaking kindness is just another problem. Practicing kindness plants seeds. At the same time send loving kindness to yourself. Imagine the sweet fruit of kindness coming down through your body from your soul.

Imagine your loved one sitting in front of you. See them. Sense them. Feel them. We cannot forget the words of kindness from Princess Diana of England: "Carry out a random act of kindness, with no expectation of a reward, safe in he knowledge that one day someone might do the same for you."

Amelia Earhart told us, "A single act of kindness throws out roots in all directions, and the roots spring up and make new trees." Kindness is its own motive. We are made kind by being kind. Kindness is free. Pass it on.

Change is always painful. And change is always going to be there. Since our birth, we have changed enormously. Loss is forever present. We never know what day will be our last one to ever see some of our beloved ones.
Mark 10:27.

Most churches had Sunday School classes when I was a child. The classes were filled with the nice children. There was a little boy who came to the class. He had tattered clothes that revealed that he was quite poor. His parents never came to church. They lived in the neighborhood of the church. Their rented apartment was not far from the Western Little League Park, but nobody attended the churches within sight of their spires.

This boy's family moved because his family could not pay the rent. Their small house was owned by one of the members of one of the neighborhood churches. Of course, his clothing was not in the style of the 1950s. The popular kids wore Wenjuns' moccasins and a Madras shirt.

The other boys made fun of that little boy. This poor child had come to church on his own, wanting to know about Jesus. But the church drove him away. Our congregation had the opportunity to be kind. The church chose to be unkind and cruel to someone who could never do anything for us.

Loving kindness brings endless possibilities for our spiritual journeys. Be kind for we never know how much our grace, love, and joy will expand toward every person that we encounter during the briefs days of our lifetime.

Chapter Five

The Preaching of Kindness

When I was preaching in the chapel of the East Lake Village Care Center in Lincoln, Nebraska, a woman walked up to me after my sermon and said, "You preach with such kindness."

I simply replied, "Thank you." However, her remark was significant to me. It was a unique appraisal. I guess I had never classified my preaching as "kind." Like when a woman tells me that I look nice, I took as a compliment. It brought a smile to my face, a warmness to my heart.

The first and obvious means of communicating with kindness is through preaching. Paul stress the importance of preaching in his letter to the Romans. Romans 10:14. We have a joyful announcement to proclaim to the world. Romans 6:6-8. We are called to be the recipient of the redeeming work of Christ. We are the sources for Christ in the unkind and unredeemed people.

Kindness is an important facet of being a pastor and a preacher. Preaching is the primary task of pastoral ministry. Preaching with more kindness shows the communicator of the Good News from the Word of God incites the Spirit's gift of that fruit. Galatians 5:22. Our preaching of kindness is aligned with the superpower of God.

Preaching should illustrate the gifts of the Holy Spirit, but also the fruit of the Spirit. Kindness is not weakness. Kindness is not agreeing with everyone. The preaching of kindness does not mean that we never upset someone. Kindness is a requirement for bringing joy to the world. Titus 3:4-5. Kindness is reflected in our attitudes when we preach.

Kindness is overlooked as going beyond the delivery style. An attitude of kindness comes across in word choices, stories, and body language.

A gentle spirit and attitude reveal a kind motivation. Vulnerability is an important component of competent preaching. We preachers should smile more. Preaching is communication that uses more than words. Our movements, facial expressions, and vocal tones are important. Use your emotions. When I preach a sermon on joy, I never frown. The joy of the Lord is my strength.

The Spiritual Event of Preaching

Preaching is a spiritual event. As we listen to a lifetime of peaching, we may characterize it as fiery, stern, mean-spirited, or bad depending on the one of the text being preached. Preaching must never be unkind. The Holy Spirit comes in kindness. II Corinthians 6:6. Kindness is expressed as a command. Micah 6:8, Zechariah 7:9, Ephesians 4:32.

Kindness is not optional for effective preaching. Remember it. Love it. Put it on. Be tender and gentle. Some preachers sound like they are mad at the parishioners. I have heard such sermons as a pastor feels forced to leave.

We are to be like shepherds to comfort God's people, speak tenderly to them, and come preaching peace and forgiveness. Isaiah 40:1-2. God's kindness leads us to repentance. Titus 3:4-7. God's *hesed*, loving kindness in the Hebrew Bible, is eternal.

God has spoken in the past, now, and in the future. Preaching centers on the Word as recorded in the canonical scriptures. The Bible is our guide regarding major issues of living.

Preaching may reveal differing interpretations of the Word, but there is a discernable common faith. Reformed churches recite the Nicene Creed, which is a summary of biblical teaching. Many congregation never repeat the Nicene Creed, first written in the year 325 by an ecumenical council of the church.

Perhaps we need to redefine preaching. Some have thought that preaching as a part of our vision had to be hard, boring and doing something. Some pastors just do not want to preach.

To me, to preach is a joy. That surprising joy comes with a kind attitude and a new way of looking at ourselves. If one doesn't enjoy it, she or he leaves us and the people on earth stay cold, unmoved, and untouched.

My service as a preacher and a writer is grace, love, and joy. It is being who I am. Jeremiah 29:11. As we travel through our lives, I do pray that I am becoming the person that God had in mind when I was created. Preaching gives many varied experiences, some pleasant and enjoyable and full of delight. Some days communication of the things of God bring pain and sorrow and broken relationships.

Life is as it is. Still, I ask why things have been so difficult for me. In the story of *The Sound of Music*, the daughter of the father captain says, "Somewhere in my youth or childhood, I must have done something good."

When I think of my own life, I think that I must have done something bad.
Even when our church appointments and callings, we continue on with our lives when life is impossible. Many of my pastor friends have relationship difficulties.

Perhaps we think that our love depends on the feelings we face as we deal with others. All we can do is to respond in love. Preaching, Harry Emerson Fosdick said is similar to group counseling. Our interactions with others whether we are preaching to millions or just one other person, are based on real love for them, even when I feel so uncomfortable myself.

Preachers sometimes focus on things that are painful, sad, and difficult instead of things al around us that give us joy. Most of the time our clergy support groups spend so little time sharing the joys of preaching in a church family. Does God attend our leadership groups? Joy is the infallible sign that God is present. Our group's goal should be to help each other to become more aware of things that give us joy. Kindness dwells deep where we least expect it. Depending on the presence of kindness reveals something deep in the soul.

We must try to be like Jesus who "came preaching." Don't miss the joy that surrounds us. Preachers and others must choose not to spend too much time dwelling on distress, sadness, and past wounds. Filling ourselves with the joy of the Lord, even in the midst of sadness, gives us reasons to burst into song.

The daughter of a pastor in Waco, Texas once asked a pertinent question.
"Dad, how do we sing the sad songs of life?" Kindness has a gentle sound that bring warmth and imagination. Effective preachers bring the prophetic words to enable souls to hear, even in the silence of our calling.

Time haunts us as it slips through our fingers. Age brings the speeding of our time left. We strain against the erosion of our lives. Maybe one reason most of us preachers hold onto and keep every sermon manuscript or notes, our sermons on tape or video. We want something eternal to be harvested as we disappear from our creations of a permanence.

The shape of our souls is individual and mysteriously unique. Each is a divine masterpiece. We were dreamed about before we were born.

Each person has a unique destiny. Each has something special to do. If somebody else could do it, they would be living on earth, not us. I find joy in what God called me to do. It has been interesting and rich with unexpected rewards.

No vocation is without difficulties. Pastoring and preaching require risk that will cause pain and suffering. Everything you have done was against the grain of our culture. The soul is haunted by alternative lives we will never have. Being content with our calling makes for a richer and joyful life.

Energy is vast and immediate in the life of any minister. The passion is clear and creative. Imagination evokes horizons that will balance kindness and challenge that brings integrity to the soul.

If we act on God's loving kindness, we will have nothing to regret.

Chapter Six

The Joy of Kindness

Small acts of kindness, when multiplied by millions, bring joy to the world. Remember the last time this happened to you. As I think of my own journey through life, I find countless moments where the unexpectedness, the suddenness of an experience of kindness shook me awake. Joy measures our time by its depth, not its length.

Unexpected acts of kindness has completely changed many days. A sense of connection and joy comes each morning as we pray that ourselves, those close to us health and happiness. Spontaneous acts of kindness will be easier.

As I sit near the window of my writing office, I take in the warm sunshine and the brilliant skies. I wait for the water kettle to finish its boiling for my cup of green tea.

I pay attention. I expect the magic in the joys of kindness. I trust my life despite the traumatic times of drama. I flourish even in a world that feels unsafe and unsettling. Nature has reliable rhythms. When I walk out in nature, I am reminded to yield more, to flow with the movement of life rather than fighting against it. Clear out the old say the Nebraska winds. Stay the course. Never weaken or you'll be blown away.

Jesus says that God will take care of the tiny sparrows flitting from branch to branch above their new homes. If God cares so much for sparrows, imagine what a treasure you must be. I can think of fettering my own nest with things that bring me joy. I know I was created in blessing and called to live in light. We were created to mirror the integrity of God.

Kindness of friends, family, and colleagues keeps us going when throws barriers or challenges in our way. Joy makes those good moments radiate.

There is something about an act of kindness from an unexplained source that causes its rippling to be especially powerful. Life without joy is no life at all. Isaiah 55:12.

When we focus attention on pain and suffering, we miss the opportunities that are all around us to be surprised by joy. Joy is an infallible sign of God's presence. Joy might not be overly exuberant. Quiet joy just under the surface may be just what we have been looking for. Softness in the breeze, the songs of birds, or seeing babies sleeping in peace brings us delight.

Writing a biography of joy is a powerful way to help us look at our lives in positive ways. Joy brings acceptance and self-confidence. Begin back when you were a child. Joy felt good in your little body. As you grew order the things that brought you were Christmas mornings, family trips, birthday celebrations, and first loves. As a teen, you felt joy after accomplishing a skill as during a piano recital, or the times you felt close to your mother or father. The joy of kindness is essential for healthy living.

Consider joy as a dose of vitamin J for your life wellness. The kindness of others is revealed for the gift it is. In an act of kindness, we expand ourselves. By naming and sharing our joy, we experience feelings of composure and contentment.

Kindness has gracious eyes. It is not a competitive fruit. Kindness casts a differing light of empathy. To be born is to be chosen.

All during his early life, C.S. Lewis sought to experience joy. He failed to create it. He failed to make it come to him. When Lewis trusted Jesus that brought salvation, he was surprised by joy. He had no expectation. Yet, joy hugged him and held him.

Joy comes as we get close and intimate with God. Never underestimate the possibilities for positive change and growth wrought by the joy of kindness.

Joy comes in the morning and surprises us. It touches us. It supplies that missing ingredient that satisfies our longings. Joy comes in friendships, as someone special cares about us. There is no right way to be kind. We all have our individual ways. There are influenced by our culture, gender, and upbringing. Touch and actions speak more clearly than words.

During those experiences, we discover a small gesture, a friendly greeting, a smile, and the help of strangers. I once did family therapy in the homes of people who lived in Lincoln, Nebraska. Many people found it hard to get their children or themselves to come into the offices of licensed psychotherapists working for Cedars Home for Children.

I served there for five years. I had a difficult time finding some of the poor families with serious problems. Sometimes I felt lost in the city. I brought a city map along. One day, I was just about to give up, and a random stranger offered her help. She pointed out the way to where my client family lived.

Kindness brings us a complete change from feeling stressed to feeling an elation and connection with the world. I could only give what I had to give. I gave Christmas presents and food from my church food bank, strengthening the power of my kindness.

We all have the potential to be kind. However, we must practice it to bring our potential to fruition. Just like a muscle can be trained by lifting weights, people can build their kindness.

Surprising joys happen in challenging moments. It is possible. It is essential to preserve. In my books on joy, I illustrate how joy happens. We must be intentional if we desire to experience unexpected joy when life takes a turn we never saw coming.

Difficult seasons bring challenging situations. Some have back-to-back seasons. When it rains, it pours. During my vision quest for living a joyful life, I find surprises. James 1:1-4. I spark joy to lift my own and others' spirits to get through difficult times. After my wife's surgery for breast cancer, she had to undergo chemical therapy. In the infusion room, the song, "Here Comes the Sun" by the Beatles. Songs of empowerment bubble up in troubling times bring magic. Joy helps create emotional resilience.

Our One Precious Life

Life is of short time. Each moment is precious. We must drop our preoccupations and pretense and freshly take in the wonder that exists all around us. Life has a beginning, middle, and end. It is not how long we live, but it's how deeply and fully we live.

The joy of kindness is not a passive experience. We deliberately invest our lives with joy. As we practice kindness, others will notice and respond in kindness. Amazingly, we link our value and our worth with productivity and our performance. Often, we become what we do. Inactivity causes us to question our value. Older and retired ministers question themselves. We are vulnerable during the times we are waiting to be love for who we are and not for what we do.

Our old mental tapes tell us this time of inactivity is wrong. So we fill our time with more doing. We sense that soul-work is being done as God conceives newness in the silence within.

The song of our soul lures us to the edge of action. On the edge of our sacred journey, memories and stories become our teachers. We stand at the edge of all our hopes and dreams. We listen to the voice of God.

My times of surprising joy has informed me about the value of kindness. After a full morning of writing, I decided to give myself a time for lunch. I drove downtown Lincoln and found a nice restaurant in a mall. I had to stan to wait for a table. While I was waiting, three lovely women were on the waiting bench. I felt a bit anxious as I smiled at them. One said that there was room to wait with them. We talked a little and their table was called. After being seated one woman came back to me. She asked me to join. A bit of satisfaction and joy quietly touched me inside.

The women ordered their lunch. I told the waiters that my order was separate. We chatted, shared our lives, laughed, and enjoyed that time. Their kindness brought joy to me.

In our lives everyone is so busy. Ordinary people can bring us joy. These wholesome ladies left a kind mark. As they were about to leave, one of them asked me if I wanted a box for the remainder of my lunch. She flashed her clear blue eyes and smiled and told me that they had paid for my meal. Their grace and kindness touched me.

The Power of Kindness in Small Specific Joys

When described in general terms, joy might elude us. Specific little joys allow us to get a clear picture. For example, when we describe the joy of a corgi in yellow rain shoes is more meaningful than saying my puppy gives me a warm joy.

We use specificity when communicating joy. Pay attention to textures, scents, and sounds that are unusual. Joy comes in tiny packages. Joy is coming home and seeing a new bunch of flowers blooming in your backyard. Joy is revealed when we see five automobiles of the same color in a row. Joy is eating fresh strawberries or tomatoes off the vine. Having a leaf fall on or in front of us just to give a kind hello. When bus drivers wave to each other as they pass. Watching a grandson concentrate on a difficult task. Coming home after dark and in the glowing windows seeing your family. Sitting inside your dirty car at a carwash. Walking along and the crossing turns green without our breaking stride. Hearing a favorite song end as you arrive home. These are small but specific joys.

Different types of music trigger sensations in distinct parts of our bodies. We move our arms and legs to the music. We enjoy these tangible physical sensations

The joy came as a gift, a gift of time. We never saw each other again.

The Unexpected Consequences of Kindness

Only eternity will reveal the full impact of being kind. Kindness improves our well-being. Kindly buying a cup of coffee will boost our mood. Kindness does not always bring the realization of how much of an impact it makes.

Human connection brings on kindness. The connection does not depend on the number of friends, or if we are living in committed relationships. Quality matters.

The unexpected consequences are soaking in a morning birdsong, remembering a cherished memory, looking at photos in a life album, listening to music linked to a special moment.

My tastes in music differ as I grow older. Lower blood pressure, reduced anxiety, improved sleep quality, and enhanced mood are examples of unexpected consequences.

Experiencing joy in the light of difficult times results from some easy modifications in our daily activities. We can let joy be in our journey.

As the Texas A and M University reads, "There shall be no regrets." When we come to the end of life, we will have some regrets. We would like to do things over again. Imperfection is the inescapable part of living as a human being. If you are a mother or a father, I know you are thankful for your children. I thank God for my daughter. Fifty-three years ago, she was placed in my arms for the first time. Her tiny fingers curled around mine. Her big blue eyes opened and sometimes searched for me as she listened to her mom's young voice. Her skin was soft and supple and had the fragrance of our firstborn child. I really loved her, even in my imperfection as her dad. I am now grateful for her uniqueness. If I had created her, she might be completely different. I might have created her based on my needs. She was created in God's image, so she could face the sorrows and joys in her life. She knows who she is as a wife and mother. Her home is filled with gladness. She prepares meals for her family. She helps mend broken hearts. She corrects her son out of her love.

Today, she is a successful woman. She has become not only my daughter, but also a valued friend.

I believe her secret to enjoy her life, her husband, and her son is living in this moment. The now. Spencer Johnson wrote about learning to live in the present. He began his book with these words, "Once there was a boy, who listened to a wise old man, and thus began to learn about the present.

The old man and the boy had known each other for a year, and they enjoyed talking to each other." (Spencer Johnson, *The Present: The Secret to Enjoying Your Work and Life, Now*, p. 13)

Conceptualize your life as a long novel. How would you write in he last chapter? We would see that many things did not work out? We are the readers, not the authors of the novel. We cannot control external events. The life story will never be perfect. Readers will see us as we are, we shall see our good intensions. These have been reflected in our words and deeds. In so doing, we need never have regrets.

I pray I share kindness wherever God sends me. I believe that God called me to be a communicator with my few skills of writing, preaching, teaching, and healing the soul. Christians call counseling "psychotherapy." From two Greek words, psyche as soul and healing. I just listen. I only give advice if asked. Long ago, I became a charter member of the American Association of Christian Counselors. I am also trained in coaching, a way of counseling that uses questions from the coach. The client answers and then another question helps them to clarify and home in on a solution to their problem.

Perhaps you might find the prayer I pray in silence as I offer the ministry of counseling. "Here I am, Lord. I claim your joy as my strength. Help me to communicate your loving kindness with my eyes and my smile. Help me show this person that there is light at the end of the therapy tunnel."

Weather the storms of life without losing connection with the Spirit of Joy. The joy of the Lord is the most effective thing we offer those in need. Allow God to bless them through your smile and your kindness.

A Christian minister is tuned in to the stirrings of the Holy Spirit. This is a spirit of humility as we ask God for guidance. Needless to worry about the past or future destroys your peace. We cannot give people advice such as "Be more joyful." Emotional relief is a product of an effective counselor or coach.

Any counselor who belongs to the American Association of Christian Counselors headquartered in Virginia is told to listen to the soul of a person. Souls are held hostage if they think in terms of a child-parent relationship. Every relationship has to be adult-to-adult.

We cannot live in a fantasy world. Some people require reality therapy before they can be awakened to the consequences of staying the same. We need to take responsibility for her own safety.

Pampering is a delusion. It solves nothing. Any Pollyanna approach results in failure. Do what you have power to do. Go where the joy is. Prayer will be your strongest help. God is with us every step of the way.

Even the strongest of individuals find it difficult to change a negative pattern of thinking that has become a habit. They don't know how to erase the tape.

The joy of kindness gives life meaning. It will reward us in due time. The joy of the Lord is living in you. Loving kindness delights you. God loves you. Listen to the Holy Spirit. The spirit is the source of love, strength, and joy.

Pray for the serenity to accept the things you cannot change, the courage to change the things you can, and the wisdom to know the difference.

Chapter Seven

The Rewards of Kindness

The novelist Henry James was asked by young student what he ought to do with his life. James responded, "Three things in human life are important. The first is to be kind. The second is to be kind. And the third one is to be kind." (Lawrence Edel, *Henry James: A Life.* New York: Harper Collins, 1987, p. 43)

Kindness is its own reward. Kind deeds clearly enrich the lives of those who receive these deeds. Kindness lifts the mood of the most disheartened person. Being kind brings increased joy to the giver of these loving gestures.

Take time to reward yourself. In some families nobody ever rewards us. We were not rewarded for good behavior. We were not loved unconditionally. So we became tired, weary, not rewarded. Our passion will wane if our good is never good enough. If we feel like the world offers no reward to you, it might be because you are not rewarding yourself. Reward yourself by allowing yourself to enjoy what you give yourself, or what you are now doing.

Being aware that our lives are finite enriches each day we live. The reward of wisdom comes from this awareness. When we are in the midst of difficult times, we must remind ourselves that we need to focus our attention on now. Don't forget.

When we face dark and trying times, we find it difficult to be kind. When I walked into a home in Lincoln to share my soul-healing, I noticed the father had a gun on his bed in the one-room abode. Most therapists descend into negativity and feelings of frustration, distress, and anxiety. I knew the plight and the hardship of this family gave perspective to this difficulty.

To navigate the marathon journey of being a physician, therapist, nurse, or minister, self-compassion and kindness to oneself is essential. Mistakes will happen. These do not define us.

Despite the dysfunctional and negative thoughts in our brains, our brains can be rewired to think more kind thoughts. The rewards of Christ are unsearchable. Ephesians 3:18. God draws us with rewards from kindness. We share in God's generous rewards.

Transcending Limitations

We are free now. We put limitations on ourselves. Our prisons are our making. Do not blame yourself. God is trying to break you out of prison. Set yourself free. Go on a life journey of grace, love, and joy as your rewards. New dreams and new people will be there for you. Cherish the moments to grow and learn. We need to break through our own resistance. What we resist is what we need the most.

There are borders and barriers to cross. Those barriers are mostly within us. We need to embrace the surprise experiences, the mysteries of life as they unfold. Do what you have the power to do to break through resistance.

Relationships do not end with death. Our children, our spouses and everybody who has loved us become a part of us, and we are part of them.
We continue to influence our thoughts, actions, and feelings. Healing and wholeness are rewards of kindness.

Being complete in our relationships, we feel whole, at peace, with no regrets. Kindness helps us attain completion. It's accompanying joy renews the circle of our most cherished relationships. Relationships involve two people. You can only deal with your part in it.

Determination is the key to recovery from illness, physical or mental. It takes time to do what you can each day, and to leave what you cannot do for tomorrow. Decide and declare that you will be whole. The biggest issue is the quality of your life.

A thankful man drove through to share rewards with others by paying for the meals at McDonald's for a car behind his. He told the rewarded receivers to pass it on. Two hours later, more than 100 cars received a paid-for meal. They had volunteered to pay for those behind them.

What happens with acts of kindness is amazing. God has been generous with divine rewards of kindness. So reward others with your kindness.

At the end of life, we all need is to hear if there life made a difference. They need to know that they made a contribution. When we are able to accept kindness, a wonderful sense of resolution occurs.

Kindness is a way of seeing, of being, and contentment. It is a response of our inner wisdom to our accumulated confusion. Permit me to share a few words from *Qualities*. ("Kindness) wears Saturn's rings on the fingers of her left hand. She is intimate with the life force. She understands the meaning of sacrifice. She is not afraid to die. There is nothing you cannot tell her. Kindness speaks with a slight accent. She was a vulnerable child, miserable in school, cold, sly, alert to the pain in the eyes of classmates. The other kids teased her about being too sentimental, and for a long time she believed them. In the ninth grade she was befriended by courage.

"Courage lent kindness bright sweaters, explained the slang, showed her how to play volleyball, taught her you can love people and not care what they think about you. Kindness is still the stranger, neither wonderful, nor terrible, herself, utterly, always." (J. Ruth Gendler, *Qualities*, p. 23)

Rewards of kindness have enjoyed a boom, beginning with the "practice random acts of kindness" movement for the last 30 years. "Be kind" signs are seen in practically every city. People continue to be unkind. Meanness and harshness prevail. The pandemic has caused us to be anxious. To understand kindness, we begin with God. Later in this book, I'll write about "*hesed,*" the Hebrew word for "loving kindness."

I wrote this book to teach other people the value of kindness. Of course, kindness is its own reward. I was rewarded in that my own understanding of kindness has deepened. Kindness has remarkable impact.

Each generation blames the older generation for making mistakes and doing and saying the wrong things. My own parents were called "the greatest generation." My parents made sacrifices, endured hardships, and worked to do all they could. Our parents were not perfect. Neither are we. Parenting remains a humbling experience. Being a good parent never has required perfection. That makes practicing kindness so important.

Aging, illness, and caregiving is what we can expect in tidal waves. There will be more old people than young people. In the past, humans died quickly from lung, heart, liver, kidney disease, and cancer. Today, people live on for years.

Rewards from the Practice of Kindness

The rewards from practicing kindness will make us more loving and stronger. We will feel self-confident, we will be delighted in and feel accepted by the world, which will reward us with an affinity which transforms us with all others.

Kindness rewards include the body's natural response to stress with small acts of kindness. Both kindness to others and kindness toward ourselves rewards us with better health. Kindness is an antidote to stress.

When my wife suffered from breast cancer, she strengthened her connections and felt supported in her continuing kindness. Kindness helps us live longer. We are rewarded by being softer and having improved moods. Cultivating warmth toward others and self-compassion toward ourselves had extraordinary rewards.

Kind people do not intentionally do kindness to receive rewards. They do it for feeling natural joy and well-being. Please be kind to yourself. Have mercy. We may think we are at fault.

It's Not Your Fault.

One thing I clearly remember that Dr. James Reilly told my wife Laurel before surgery was, "It is not your fault."

We have been rewarded with people who love us, but unless we feel a sense of our worthiness, you cannot feel that abundant love. We could feel isolated, alone, or unworthy.

Physical frailty is not a sign of personal or moral weakness. In these ungraceful circumstances, dignity resides in recognition of our predicament and gracious acceptance of help from others.

You have now become the designated ill person in your family. Loved ones will be rewarded by spending time with you. Connect. Spend the time. Some avoid people in their final years, because we worry that death is contagious. Don't worry. We are all infected. Nobody will get out of this life alive.

Love conquers all even in situations that are unimaginable. Paul wrote, "But the greatest of these is love." John Lennon sang, "All you need is love." Love knows no bounds. It is an impulse that is transcendent. It is the same in a child's love for her parents. We belong to one another, and that is the best part of being alive.

Into our older years past 80, we still might drive a car, clean our home, cook, and even start a new job like substitute teaching. Some are active and independent in their ninth decade. Age will take its toll. Arthritis, failing eyesight, poor hearing, and more things than we count, invade our lives.

The sadness of our coming deaths will continue to be there. Intense joy will also be with us in ways in which people connect in those final days. The burden of love does not stop. At times it is difficult and demanding.
Be inspired as you see kindness in a differing view.

When we view spring flowers on a hillside, we are surprised in their beauty. These flowers differ in size, color, and shape. Our God of beauty makes us strong and attractive, clothed with delight.

Several loving friends and family bought spring flowers to cheer my wife Laurel during the days of recovering from cancer. Laurel enjoys her own flower garden.

I saw the flowers as loving rewards for all that Laurel has meant in her places and peoples she has encountered in the world.

The best kind of joy comes in our awareness of love. The reward comes richer as you are doing kindness. Embrace the mystery of life. Let yourself experience life. Feel everything you need to feel. Feel the sun on your shoulders.

Watch the magical life journey unfold with all its ups and downs. Feel your awareness rise up from deep within and grasp the insights as they come.

One of my recent joys in older age is to write all my books with the Holy Spirit as my guide. There is that human joy that every writer feels during the process of creating a new piece of literature. The joy of the Lord is my strength. That joy comes from the knowledge that I am actually co-writing this book with the Holy Spirit.

The weakness in my writing, grammatical errors, poor choices of words, and awkward sentences are my own responsibility. The Holy Spirit gives me the self-drive and inspiration to share my creations. I am so grateful for this interaction. I feel God's grace beyond understanding. I respond to God as my lover within. This also is beyond my understanding. God delights in loving us. God never leaves my side. Acts 17:28.

Our inner joy will find a way to express itself in our words and in our appearance. Proverbs 15:13. A smiling heart is a soul glowing in love.

We are rewarded with peace and harmony of body, mind, soul, and spirit. If we choose to be kind and grateful. We will all experience pleasures, contentment, and bodily comforts. We know that we are loved.

The joys of the body are precious. Sexual pleasure is a good gift of God. Sex outside of marriage, or sex tat abuses another person is degrading and sinful. Some churches teach that any sexual pleasure is degrading. They think our bodies are evil, and the soul is good.

Sexuality is connected to our souls. Let go of sexual shame. Embrace your sensuality. To some sex is a spiritual problem. Sex is an amazing way to open our senses: touch, smell, seeing, tasting, and hearing.

Jesus did not come to turn us against our own bodies. Unbridled sexual desire and activity is lustful. Good and kind sex that is practiced artfully within marriage is beyond ecstasy. Sexual intimacy is the outward sign of the commitment to love.

Joys of the body are precious. Sexual intimacy connected to love is both graceful and grace giving. Sex elevates the body and also the spirit and the soul. Sex opens us to appreciate colors, scents, textures, and sounds.

Be done with sexual shame. Trust your body. We are not disconnected parts. Open up. See my book on sexuality published by Parson's Porch books. The title is *The Silence of the Church: The Spiritual Struggle with Sexuality*. Sexual intimacy serves as a resource for spiritual transformation and renewal. Making love can be a delightful means of grace. My book addresses the issue of the traditional sexual ethics. Sex with the right person which is your lawfully wedded spouse. Most committed partners see their boundaries final, fixed, and absolute.

The spiritual struggle with sexuality includes any reflections on proper sexual conduct. Our preaching, teaching, and counseling shows little concern with things such as love, consent, mutual pleasure, tenderness, kindness, intimacy, and joy.
Sexuality is God's gift that involves our body, our intellect, our will, and our soul. Honor it in your ministry.

Exercise Brings the Intellect to Life

Every day we should move our bodies with exercise. Walking is better than running. Exercise ignites the sparks in your brain's engine. Feeding and training our bodies builds muscles, tendons, ligaments, bones, hearts, and lings, and our brains

Our Intellect, Will, and Soul

The intellect and the will are parts of the soul. The will decides what thoughts the mind will think. For as we think, we will behave. The will controls our decisions. The mind gathers the facts. The will can say yes or no.

Taking good care of the soul means that we do what is necessary to become our own best friend. To be fully alive is to be physically, emotionally, and spiritually healthy. It is important that we decide to join God early in our lifetime.

Our wills say yes. So we are moved toward the right direction. Your willful yes is the whole foundation and power to change. We sometimes think there are people whom we will never get along with. Some you simply detest. Matthew 5:46. God will give us the grace to get along with everyone you encounter in your personal life.

The key is our will to say yes. All things are possible. Changes that make life better will produce good fruit. The soul helps us relate to our inner world by helping us love our neighbors as we are loving ourselves. God and the things of God become like the air we breathe.

If we decide to fill our souls with love, we will not keep our poor thinking. We will keep out the negativity. Our eyes are the windows of our souls. I Corinthians 2:9.

Accept Jesus, accept the Holy Spirit and the tied together love of the trinity. When the soul is directed in loving kindness, joy bubbles to the surface from the depths of your soul. The rewards are remarkable.

I constantly collect loving kindness phrases in my personal vision quest to come fully alive.

May I be free from danger.
May I have mental happiness.
May I have physical happiness.
May I have the ese of well-being.
(Sharon Salzberg, *Lovingkindness: The Revolutionary Art of Happiness*)

May I feel protected and safe.
May I feel content and pleased.
May my physical body provide me with strength.
May my life unfold smoothly with ease.
(Sylvia Boorstein, *Pay Attention, For Goodness Sake: The Buddhist Path to Kindness*)

May I and all beings be filled with lovingkindness.
May I and all beings be safe from inner and outer dangers.
May I and all beings be well in body and mind.
May I and all beings be happy and free.
(Jack Kornfield, *The Art of Forgiveness, Lovingkindness, and Peace)*

May I be well and happy.
May I be strong, confident, and peaceful. May I have ease and well- being.
(Andrew Weiss, *Beginning Mindfulness*)

May I be filled with lovingkindness.
May I be held in lovingkindness.
May I accept myself just as I am.
May I be happy.
May I touch great and natural peace.
May I know the natural joy of being alive.
May my soul and mind awaken.
May I be free.
(Tara Brach, *Radical Acceptance: Embracing Your Life with the Heart*)

Chapter Eight

The Practice of Kindness

Kindness is a lifestyle. It is a choice. As Christian believers we are to grow in the fruit of the Spirit. Growth takes time and energy. A seed does not transform into a tree overnight. With careful watering, tending, and patience, a seed will slowly grow into a towering tree. It is the same as practicing kindness.

Think about the kind people in your life and how they make you feel. Recall the warm glow in your soul every time you think of them. Kindness lingers when you are facing your difficult challenges. Kindness lives in our souls forever.

The practice of remembering the Golden Rule will nurture our relationships. Treating others like we want to be treated gives us incredible power to gather insights and to transform our interactions. Psalm 116:2.

Make a habit of focusing on kindness. Every one can cultivate a natural habit of kindness. Focus on kindness every day for a month. You will see joyful changes in your life. You will feel so much better as a person. Being kind is karma in practice.

Being kind should be in our daily mission. It is our habit of goodness. It requires intentionality. We tend to want to choose whom we show our kindness to. Kindness lowers its eyes and look at those below, who have nothing, can offer nothing. Jesus was always selfless. He turned nobody away. Kindness is the practice of doing something good and not expecting anything in return. Luke 11:18.

Love requires will power. Feelings wear away with time. For a marriage to last for even ten years or so, it takes the will to bear discomfort, to be willing to forgive, and the ability to laugh.

No matter how perfect you think your marriage is, the relationship is between two incompatible people. Couples bind themselves together for life.

Remaining faithful to their promises and agreeing to raise children takes all the energy that we have. Each human being is unique. Likewise, every couple is incompatible in differing ways. After being married 50 or 60 years, we remain mysteries to each other. Patience, perseverance, and the will to keep the love alive are required.

Successful couples hang in there. The will to endure all things keeps a marriage from falling apart. For love to flourish, the couple must pay a heavy price. Miracles are possible.

Zechariah 7:9-10 summarizes how kindness looks. We need to practice kindness now. Kindness is the quality of being generous, friendly, considerate, and respectful. Unkindness looks mean, rude, disrespectful, and violent. Unkindness is often loud, obnoxious, demeaning, and insulting.

Kindness Looks Like Christ.

Kindness looks like Christ. It is a continual practice. We can be Jesus to someone today and every day. Make Christ your role model and kindness your lifestyle. Jesus practiced the disposition we should have toward others. It is more than a feeling. It is a fruit or a quality that causes us to act in a kind manner. Colossians 3:1-12.

Being kind has a chain reaction. We learn as we watch others. In practicing kindness, we have to be intentional. It is one thing to be taught kindness. It is another thing to be touched by it.

Missing the importance of warmness stands in our way of being kinder. Most people do desire to perform kind actions.

Underestimating the impact of kindness reduces the likelihood of carrying out warm kind behaviors.

Every human soul is a medium through which God's nagnetism flows. Unkindness obstructs the power. We must be loving and kind to all persons. Unkindness drowns out love. Practicing the end of unkind words protects our lives from the invasion of trouble and unexpected partings.

Kindness liberates us. Deep kindness brings inward peace. We accept all things without judgment. We look with kindness of every person. Being kind to other folks helps us practice the art of being kind to ourselves.

Being kind to ourselves prevents burn-out and disillusionment. Embrace contradictions and inconsistencies. Be empowered to treat others with loving kindness.

God calls us to have the fruit of kindness as a purposeful, intentional, routine part of living as followers of Christ. God is kind. Psalm 145:17. God laments like a loving parent over the refusal to be kind. Hosea 11:4.

Jesus describes how kind God is. Luke 6:35-36. We are to imitate the kindness of God. Practicing Christ's likeness means being kind to others even when they are not kind to us. Proverbs 11:17. Practicing kindness results in feeling better about ourselves. Practicing kindness means more kindness. For the faithful, love is alive. Colossians 3:12-13.

Unkindness is an indigestion. If we decide to practice changes, start by speaking sincere kind words to those to whom you have been harsh. Wear the garment of courteous language. The joy of the Lord is our strength for holding the reins over the wild steeds of our temper by calm silence. Kind words are more powerful than people's ugliness.

Practice respect and courtesy to avoid negative vibrations. With a little kindness on our part, we find it possible to find accommodations. Relationships require practice. Learn to be courteous to close relatives, and we will be habitually kind to all people.

Respect is a spiritual power. It helps us free ourselves. Respect and honor yourself. Respect the needs of your body, mind, and soul. Respect the vision quests of others. Respect the gifts of life. Bow in spirit to each person you meet. Discover the power of respect. Practice it often.

Kind words are nectar to thirsty souls. Vibrations of words are so powerful that if we live in the same building with people who hold unhealthy thoughts, which will affect us.

Kindness is incredible. People can pass on kindness as they watch others do kind deeds, and as they receive kindness. Kind people live longer. They function better and they realize that their life matters.

Saint Paul wrote of the incomprehensible kindness of God for people who are lost. Romans 11:22, Titus 3:1-7. Kindness the quality of understanding sympathy and concern for those in trouble or need. It is demonstrated in our speech, conduct, and forgiveness of injuries sustained. Psalm 141:5.

Shining for God with Secret Acts of Kindness

Jesus told us that our motivation for doing acts of kindness is to please our Lord. Matthew 5:16, 6:1-4. To offer yourself into God's service to use us for the glory of God. During my retirement ministry years, I have continued to preach and sing in homes where older people live. Louisville Care Center, Good Samaritan Center and Linden View Center in Syracuse, and the East Side Village Care Center in Lincoln have continued to bring me joy. My motivation is not to help me look good, but to obey and please God.

A few severely crippled seniors were sitting outside in wheelchairs. Every congregation where I have been appointed or elected as pastor has had a ministry to nursing homes and care centers. Some felt they had been forgotten by the church. Some residents were still members of the church I represented.

The practice of kindness extends to many levels of living. Never underestimate the power of kindness and our ability, strengthened by grace, to lead people into a life of joy. Practicing kindness will cause us to be kind. That is what I mean when I say kindness is contagious.

As we do unto others, they reciprocate to us. We reach down into that part of us that is kind. Kindness is our way of seeing beyond the present. Colossians 3:7. We are kind as the work of Christ enables us to be kind.

Taking communion with those who miss the opportunity of sharing it with other believers had become a rare gift of grace, love, and mercy.

Heaping with Burning Coals

Howard Thurman was an advisor and mentor of Martin Luther King, Jr.
Thurman was born into an African American family of sharecroppers on a farm. His home was near the home of some white sharecroppers.

Soon after my family moved in, our white neighbor cleaned out their chicken coop. They threw manure over he fence that separated their backyards. Thurman and his family became irate at this insult.

He and his parents left that huge pile of chicken manure out in the hot summer sun. As fall arrived, they dug up a pile of earth. They worked the chicken manure into the soil. As spring came, they turned their land over again and planted some seeds.

About the first of June, the family harvested fresh flowers and delicious looking vegetables and placed them in a cart.
Those white sharecroppers had never spoken to us. His mom pushed the cart around the little fence between their backyards up to the porch of the neighbors' house. She knocked on the door. Surprised to see her, she kindly said, "Thank you for sharing your chicken manure with us last summer. Now I want to share my flowers and vegetables with your family."

We are supposed to treat each other with kindness. We are to treat even those who hurt us with loving kindness. Ephesians 4:32. These two families crossed the racial division and became friends.

We recognize kindness when we experience it. Glen Campbell wrote a hit song, "If you try a little kindness, then you'll overlook the blindness, of the narrow-minded people, on the narrow streets."

Kindness operates on the principle of the harvest. We reap more than what we sow. When we sowed potatoes one spring to add to our food bank, we saw that one potato yields handfuls of nice potatoes.

One act of kindness evokes other acts of kindness. Philippians 2:3-5. Kindness blindness needs to be restored. Our eyes have numerous cones and rods that interpret blue, green, and red colors. Color blindness is the inability to differentiate certain colors.

That is a metaphor of what Christ Jesus has done for us. He restores the image of God in us. Titus 3:45. Jesus told us that kindness is what God is like. God is kind to the selfish sinners and those who are not grateful. Luke 6:35.

The fruit of kindness does not come from the human spirit. It comes from the Holy Spirit. The fruit of the Spirit is like God. Jesus told us to be like God. Kindness is not based on someone's worthiness. Kindness is not an easy thing to do. Scripture tells us to "put on" kindness just as put on a coat. And like your warm winter coat, kindness is what people see on the outside. Kindness will show if it is present. Micah 6:8.

It is so much easier to hurt someone's feelings than to show kindness. To tell of another's faults is easier than being kind. Luke 6:35.

Living the Kindness of God

Kindness is like love. It does not mean avoiding difficulty. Kindness and compassion serve as the place to confront those we love.

We all have sin blindness. Jesus came to lead us beside still waters, restoring our souls. Jesus came to us in the incarnation from the riches of heaven. He became poor for us so we could become rich toward God. He is the embodiment of kindness.

Kindness in Difficult Situations

We are tempted to be unkind in difficult situations. In a million little ways, we are given the option and the opportunity to show kindness. Be gentle with yourself when you believe you are stuck. You need a new and fresh viewpoint.

Respect your darker moments, the difficult times when you become uncertain. Respect the timing as your life and journey unfolds.

Journal Prompts for Practice of Kindness

Journal about a challenging situation. What caused it to be difficult? How was it handled?

Write two things that someone has done for you in the last week?

Reflect on experiences where you were able to be specially kind to another person.

Recall a time when you behaved unkindly to someone.

When has someone helped you so much that you feel like crying tears of gratitude?

Journal about experiences that taught you how to give back kindness to the world.

Think of someone you dislike. Look and listen closely to how she thinks and behaves.

Journal about points in the day that you need a boost of kindness.

Write your self three compliments. Say thank you to yourself for making your own joy.

Think about the positive changes you would like to see in this world. What do you think would happen if everyone started to act kinder to one another?

A young woman named Michelle shed tears as she walked from a jewelry store that told her it would cost her $500 to replace a lost diamond in her wedding ring. She spotted a boy. He looked lost and this lad was weeping too. She reached out to attempt to comfort him. Michelle offers loving kindness. Jesus' kindness is about attitudes and actions that encourage people and solve their problems.

Michelle was in no mood to be kind, but she made the decision to do it. Kindness is not the same for everybody. As a poor ministerial student at Carson-Newman University in Jefferson City, Tennessee, I did not own a car. Hitch-hiking was common in those days. Everybody used the method.

After more than 60 years since I was there, I am still touched by the kindness of strangers. We are still called to notice need and frustration. Intentional acts of kindness brighten our unkind world. It lifts and encourages people to love one another.

Fanny Crosby, who wrote many of our favorite hymns, described how sometimes, in the human soul, there are feelings that can be "wakened by kindness."

We may not have experiences of dramatic conversions when we do kindness evangelism. It is enough that we can be with people with our gifts of love. As with any kind of evangelism, we place all the results into the loving kindness hands of God.

A nurse named Christie Watson wrote a wise and tender novel about the joys and the difficulties of being kind to others at their most vulnerable and how to care better for the nurses who care for us. (Christie Watson, *The Language of Kindness: A Nurse's Story*, 325 pages.

My wife Laurel served as a nurse for about 60 years. She is the kindest person I have ever known. The following anonymous prayer says it all.

As I care for my patients today, be there with me, God, I pray. Make my words kind. In my hands place your healing touch.

Let your divine love shine through all that I do. May others see you inside of me.

Give me kindness, compassion, and understanding. Give me skill and tenderness. Give my ears, the ability to listen. Give to my lips words of comfort.

Give me strength for my selfless service. Enable me to give hope to hose that I serve. Lord help me to bring comfort where there is pain. Give me courage where there is fear. Give hope where there is despair. Give me acceptance when the end is near. Amen.

While I am living on earth, I want to practice loving kindness. In my ninth decade of life I look forward with joyful anticipation to the day that I meet Jesus face to face.

The nearer I get to that glorious occasion, the less worthy I believe I am. I pray my defects, shortcomings, and failures as I count on the mercy of God. With intimate prayer and works of kindness during my short life, I will enjoy my final days.

Chapter Nine

The Prayers of Kindness

Prayer causes us to be intimate with God. When God lives in us, we become instruments of kindness. Praying people have kind hearts. With the image of God, we become more like Christ. Prayer gives us the fuel to practice kindness to other people.

God always answers our prayers. When the answer is not what we wanted or asked for, the Lord gives us a much better gift. The assurance is found in the incarnation. God lived among us in Jesus Christ. He will never depart when we need him. Right now, in this moment, Jesus is with us.

Prayer is simply the name that has been given to communication, an awareness of God, a conscious being with God, being present with God, and God being present with us.

Conversation and communication are required for being in a human relationship. Developing a healthy relationship requires being with each other, talking and being aware of one another. Prayer is the word for paying attention to God. I Corinthians 2:11-12. Prayer is communication in the Holy Spirit with people we cannot see in spirit. It is the reality of spiritual seeing, touching, hearing, and tasting God who is everywhere. If we do not spend time alone with God, there will be something missing.

Our faithfulness to daily prayer makes a significate difference in our following of Jesus. What I have called kindness evangelism is needed to draw people to a personal commitment to Christ so that the Holy Spirit will be released into our lives. Matthew 6:6.

The wise choice of time and place takes awhile but it is half the battle. Some thought also needs to be given as to the right time. We live in a complicated world. Consideration must be given for time to fit with your work and home, your spouse, your children, and your parents.

Nothing is more important than being with God. Things that appear urgent are inconsequential in the eternal perspective. As our commitment to God grows, God intends that our commitment to one another grows. As we love God more and more, we love one another more and more. I John 4:20-21.

God's deep desire for us is to have the joy of seeing our prayers answered. God wants us to know how to ask for things. John 15:7-8, 11. We must ask according to God's will. When we do, we can ask with confidence.

Jesus wants us to come to him in faith. Mark 10:13-16. He is making it clear how much he wants us to trust in his power, to trust in his love and kindness, to know that he wants to receive us and our requests.

The Epistle of James gives reasons prayers are not always answered. James 4:2-4, 7-10. We are to honor our parents, so our prayers will not be hindered. Isaiah 58:2-11 gives us insight into his truth. Isaiah in his poetic prophesy is saying that sin hinders prayer.

Praying people put kindness into action. Simple acts of kindness become automatic. We smile. We hold doors open. We say hello. We offer somebody a ride in our automobiles. We begin to see opportunities to be kind everywhere.

Prayers of kindness open our hearts and souls to God's healing touch. Sometimes troubling conditions simply disappears. The apostle Paul spoke of his prayers to remove a thorn. Our afflictions and weaknesses are a reality of human nature. Every single human living on earth has imperfections. These must be dealt with an attitude centered on God. Paul said, "Whenever I am weak, I am strong." Recognizing our own weaknesses, our humanity gives us the ability to find God and to live within the power of the grace of God.

During my spiritual journey, I discovered that I am often difficult to understand. Some have decided just to not tolerate me.

Some simple words we can use are natural. We can say, "I'm proud of you." Thank you for your help." "I appreciate you." "You are brave." "I love you." "You are wonderful." "You matter to me." "I love you." "I forgive you."

A Prayer to Be God's Instrument of Kindness

God of unfailing love, my life is a living testimony of kindness and forgiveness. You have redeemed me from an eternity of separation from your love. There is no way that I can earn it. I do not deserve it. Holy God, I am your kind brother. Make it my natural habit to be kind.

Give me the discernment, desire, and knowledge to use kindness toward anyone needing my help. Use me to be a leader, a catalyst for change. Amen.

A Prayer to Become the Image of Christ

Powerful Holy Spirit, I come praying to seek help with becoming more Christ-like. I feel a deep need to improve my kindness skills toward others. Lord Jesus, we know tat you came to exercise kindness in this earth.

I pray that I will be your ambassador of kindness and bring joy to the world. God, increase the kindness during my life's journey. Make me the image bearer of Christ that you have called me to be. Amen.

A Prayer for a Kind Heart

Father of compassionate kindness, your love and grace in kindness, you guide us toward our best behavior. May the Spirit enable me to please you by showing kindness and forgiveness. May my life be clearly marked by kindness.

Father, examine my soul to show me areas messed up with hatefulness and pride. I am flesh this side of heaven. I need to be cleansed by your holy touch.

Come and be the holy presence for my cleaning. Change me into a kind child in your family. Amen.

A Prayer for Becoming Gentle and Kind

God of all mercy, thank you for intervening in my life that has brought salvation. Lord, I know the price was huge. It required the death of Christ on the Roman cross.

Paying that price was not just for me, but for the people who cross my path each day. Your transformation miracle has made me loved and clothe with kindness and gentleness. Instill inside of me the kindness that I need.
Your kindness is evident through the rising of the sun and its lovely setting. Without the sun, we would all die. We are grateful for your power.

Keep your acts of loving kindness before my eyes each day. Make me an instrument of blessing in the lives of others.

Move my conscious self when I start to react in a way that is not Christ-like and worthy of the child of a King. King Jesus, be glorified through my life. Amen.

A Prayer for a Quiet Spirit of Kindness

Gracious God, it is difficult to remain silent. You have the power to keep my mouth closed. There are times o speak and times to be silent. Silence is an act of kindness. You promised that saving grace brings strength to those who wait on you. In the waiting, we are given courage.

Give me a quiet spirit of kindness as I wait for you to act. My God of enduring faithfulness, grant me a kind heart that knows when to speak and when to keep quiet. Amen.

A Prayer for Those Affected by Cancer

Dear Lord, I ask for grace to endure the challenge before me. You know I want to live. You know I do not want my body to change. I don't want to be sick. Clearly, you know why my husband and I must meet this challenge. Our current path is frightening.

God, we both would want to avoid it. Perhaps the physicians will tell us the diagnosis was wrong. We want our lives back to the way it was. Neither of us understands. We know we need to place our hands in yours. Guide us. Give us courage. Comfort us. Grace us with your loving kindness. Amen.

A Prayer of Kindness to Mean or Good People

My Lord Jesus, you have been kind to me by providing a path for me to be with you in an eternal heaven. Thank you for my family, friends, and kind spouse who loves me. You called me to love my wife as you love he church. May I demonstrate loving kindness to my wife. I pray that my kindness toward her reflects your kindness to me.

Be the instrument for me to be kind to other struggling human beings. Help me to be kind to those who are mean to me. Who ignore me. Who hurt me. Who pick on me. Help me to show them the kindness you have shown to me.

As I meditate on Jesus' story of the Good Samaritan, I wonder how I would react to that opportunity. I am really not sure. I pray that I may receive courage to freely give kindness despite my differences with any human, good or mean to me. Make me a Good Samaritan in this dark world.

Opportunities to be kind are everywhere. Never wait for somebody to be kind first. Practice unconditional kindness. Kindness is not a bargaining chip with strings attached. Lord, help me to expect nothing in return.

Give me the fruit of kindness no manner how awkward or inconvenient the situation may be. Amen.

A Prayer for Kindred Spirits

Kind God, for your joy and strength, we thank you. After the time of infusion of chemotherapy, we pray that Laurel and I are winning the battle s we observe others who can't envision an end.
Give all those fighters courage and strength. Grant us the strength to fight one more day. Dear Lord, bless these special lives. Bless them with hope.

Let the complete healing be of mind, body, and spirit. Let their hope shine a light that burns forever to honor the struggle. Comfort and strengthen family members as they are hurting too.

God, please give the surgeons and physicians strong minds and steady hands. We realize that here are no guarantees. That is the reason we are praying for a miracle.

Loving kind Lord, teach us o respect the path of others as we respect our path as well.

May we hold the fruit of patience and kindness and a soul that sings the music of joy. Amen.

A Prayer for Peace and Hope

Heavenly and almighty Father, we thank you for who you are and how you walk with us in his valley. We are so grateful that you enter into our pain and suffering.

The biblical record shows that you are near the brokenhearted and you save those who are crushed by pain.

Draw us closer to you. We give thanks for your loving kindness, and we ask for healing. Restore bodies that suffer from cancer. Be with us in our pain and emotional trauma of cancer.

Every time we hear about another loved one who has cancer, we feel lost and afraid. Help family and loved ones to know the kind things to say in love and support.

Cancer affects the entire family, friends, and church community. Help us use these moments of difficulty and pain as a way to become closer to you and to each other. Guide us in our current path so we can make the best of the worst times, finding a way to be faithful, knowing that you are there when we call.

Almighty Lord, we boldly ask for breakthroughs that will lead to more effective treatment and eventual cure of cancer. We give you the glory as you accomplish your will. Help us now to bring us to a deeper comprehension of unconditional love. Guide us in this moment. Amen.

A Prayerful Kindness Meditation

Go into your place of prayer. Settle in a comfortable position. Relax.

Take a deep breath and release. Focus on your breathing. Breathe in and out with each sensation of your body.

Picture someone close, someone toward whom you feel much love. Notice this feeling. Feel the sensation of openness, gentleness, tenderness and kindness. Relax.

As you breathe out, imagine the extending of a purple light hat holds your warm feelings from the center of your soul. Imagine the light surrounding your loved one. The light brings peace and happiness. Say these words.

May you have happiness.

May you be free from suffering.

May you experience joy and ease.

May you have happiness.

May you be free from suffering.

May you experience joy and ease.

Quietly repeat these words and remember to extend the violent light to your beloved from your soul.

Think of a time when this person was suffering. Perhaps they experienced an illness. Maybe an injury or a difficult relationship.

Notice your own feeling when you think of their suffering. Continue to visualize your loved one as you breathe. Extend your light as you exhale with a strong wish that they be free from the suffering. Say these words.

May you be free from this suffering

May you feel joy and happiness.

May you be free from this suffering.

May you have joy and happiness.

Contemplate a time when you have suffered yourself. Perhaps you experienced a conflict with somebody you care about and failed in something you wanted.

Notice your thoughts and feelings when you think of your own suffering.
Just as we wish for our loved one's suffering to end, we wish that our own suffering would end. You may visualize your own pain and suffering leaving so that you experience happiness.

Continue to imagine yourself as you breathe. Visualize the purple light emanating from you to ease the suffering. Each time you exhale, feel that light within you giving you freedom from suffering. Close by silently saying these words.

May I be free from this suffering.

May I have joy and happiness.

May I be free from this suffering.

May I have joy and happiness.

Now prayerfully visualize some person you neither like nor dislike. It might be your classmate or colleague with whom you are not familiar, a mail person, a house cleaner, or a bus driver.

Think of his person as suffering. The person may be having conflicts with loved ones, or they may be suffering from an illness. Do you feel warm and open or kind for this person? Now recite to her or him these words.

May you be free from suffering.

May you have joy and happiness.

May you be free from this suffering.

May you have joy and happiness. Enjoy your precious life. Every moment God's light shines within you.

Now prayerfully visualize a person with whom you have difficulty with. It could be a parent or a child with whom you have disagreed. It could be a co-worker.

Continue to visualize this person as you breathe. Perhaps there were times when you got along. Maybe you had completed a big job together. Maybe you belonged to the same church. Now as you bask in the joy of your open-hearted desire to ese the suffering of all people, you realize the joy happiness, and kindness in your own soul after prayerfully experienced this time of meditation.

Prayer Corrects Patterns of Kindness Blindness

Keeping your times of prayer and meditation will help you discover specific patterns that are sabotaging your relationships without you even realizing it.

Simple adjustments can eliminate bad patterns and boost our good ones. This results are what I call kindness-blindness. Kindness-blindness keeps us from getting ripped up in becoming our best selves.

Kind people have discovered darkness. Like an ardent whisper in an empty church, our pleas are swallowed by the silence. Even saints have felt boxed in and frustrated in a place with no exits. God seems distant. Intimate prayer is not a bargaining tool. We can never manipulate God's response. Perhaps we need to examine our image of God. We develop a picture of God from infanthood. That picture continues to influence us. To know how to be kind involves an enlargement of our image. Contrast the experiences and expectations of God with the biblical records.

During my many years of research and writing about our individual blind spots so we can fix them and find opportunities for us to seize them. We know the mystery of ambiguity that calls for deeper reflection on kindness. Prayer cannot change God. Pure prayer seeks to make our will conform to God's will. Listen to the silence. Kindness, grace, and love brings more silence and not speech.

We all play a role in each other's lives. As we travel along our own journey, we affect those around us. We unleash incredible power when we choose to pray for each other. A prayerful concern of others for us and us for them has a powerful effect on each of our lives. James 5:16.

Stress grabs us with a powerful grip. We feel helpless. Prayer is available assistance available to us. Prayer changes our way of thinking, as we call for God's help in our struggle.

Believing that we will receive help is a wonderful way to be faithful. The help comes from God's response to our prayer and from our own willingness to change our attitudes and thoughts.

Our thoughts determine the mood of our days. We chose to have positive thoughts. When we choose to seek the will of God, these thoughts will change the way we feel. Imagine that we are being comforted by God and held close. As we choose thoughts of comfort and joy, Our anxiety and weakness gives way to optimism and joy. We know that where God is, joy is.

We feel helpless and ineffective when we do not know how to help a friend in need. Being available to talk about problems or offering suggestions may be the kindest ways to help. When we become aware of people contending with difficulties and remind ourselves to pray for them.

We tend to forget our spiritual development takes place through every experience in life. We can ask God what can be learned through our experiences.

As we move through this earthly life, my we continue to know that our trust and faith will never go unrewarded.

Kindness does not mean we agree with everything. Prayerful times of meditation even with differences, we are able to express kind things. We are among those who decide to share kindness into the life of others.

God is not lost or hiding from us. God is with us at this very moment. We are always in the eyes of God's kind presence. Let God help us choose to bring ourselves back to the present moment.

We find God within us. During our busyness, we multitask and run in circles, trying to do what is necessary. We think that God has found no space to fit into our lives. Who has really moved away? We make special efforts to discover God is within us. God is closer to us than we are to ourselves.

Most people get bored with prayer on some occasions. We don't always feel like praying. We don't force ourselves to pray. We can depend on the Holy Spirit to pray within us.

Writing this book is a prayer for me. I feel the Holy Spirit guiding me. I know I am in the presence of God as I write. My writing ministry is one way to bring joy to the world.

Our boredom is not a sign of failure. It is normal to be bored. I can laugh at my boredom. Whenever we fall down, we must get back up. The heavenly goal is before us. We must come to realize that despite our humanness, God wants us to live in God's strength and joy.

Thoughts about being helpless cannot make us hopeless. God will help us learn how to cope. When the sun comes out, the snow melts. We can find our way out of darkness. Pray for guidance. Remember that God knows all things. Give God the credit as God has a plan for every one of us.

God is the lover within to guide us. In giving we receive, and we are rewarded. We must respond to the Inner Light in the way that we give of ourselves.

John Killinger gives us insight in one his beautiful pastoral prayers. "O God, whose kindness to us has taken forms we have never known and visited us in ways we did not see, we thank you for your endless mercies: for safety in traveling when some danger loomed; for return to health when disease threatened; for the smell of rain on dry pavement; for flowers that polka dot the landscape; for friends who rescue us from loneliness; for family members who stand by us in times of adversity; for a country where we are protected by law; for churches that still teach the ways of faith; for books that embody reflections and ideas; for Bibles that impart sacred history and understanding; for teachers who shape our lives; for sleep that restores; for play that rejuvenates; for prayer that sustains.

"Forgive us, we pray, for taking anything for granted. We hold before you today friends and loved ones who are il; families in which there is anxiety and trouble; persons who are out of work; children having difficulty at school; adults who cannot read; people addicted to drugs; persons contemplating crimes; persons in prison; persons experiencing burnout in work or faith or family life; those who are handicapped or whose health has debilitated in any way; those whose lives are painful and joyless; those who are out of communication with you.

"Let the vision of wholeness and commitment that was in Christ be in us also, and let your name be glorified here and in all the earth, for yours are the kingdom and the power and the glory forever. Amen." (John Killinger,
Lost in Wonder, Love, and Praise, 151-152)

Our vocation is rooted in the desires of our souls with God's love and grace. Once we discover it, we will be enabled to open the door to eternal joy.

Returning our gifts to God makes an exhilarating life. We are giving glory to God and becoming fully alive. We were created to be channels of love. Showing kindness to those in need will refresh your prayer life. That makes you a true disciple. We are accountable for the way we use our gifts and talents. Receiving God's bounty brings us to the point of bearing good fruit.

Even the greatest saints and prayer warriors were confused and mixed up at times, just like the rest of us. Note that all of us are sinners, and certainly all were human. Everybody has bad days. But eventually the delight of the spirit overpowered any barriers.

A personal, prayerful relationship with our Lord will put us in touch with the mother lode of joy. God wants to share with us. John 15:4.

The poor and the hungry are not easy to look upon. We are with Jesus, hidden in their distress. Matthew 25:40. To love God living in the least among us is a tremendous challenge.

Prayer rewards us with kind eyes enabling us to see the face of God in unlikely places. It is time for us to pray well. And to pray often. Prayer is communion with the mind and thoughts of God. Simply ask God to help those we love. Go for a long prayerful walk with God. As we pray, God appreciates when we are aggressive, direct, humble, simple, persistent, and imperfect.

We come to God fully human and unashamed of our humanity as we approach God who created us that way and is waiting for us to come that way. The Holy Spirit is imparting to our souls the faithfulness and desire to approach God.

When situations do not appear to be working, ask God to enable you to earnestly ask why. My own life has been full of unexplained mysteries. It is my motive to pray again and again.

I am aware that I have made mistakes. I expect to make more foolish decisions. I expect the Holy Spirit will continue to teach me more about prayer.

Know God in Deep Intimacy.

We are aware that we know God in deep intimacy. Respect that God is all powerful. We are all powerless. Believe that the plan of God for each of us will unfold in divine time.
Put yourself in the presence of God. Imagine that the Almighty is speaking directly to you. Absorb that God is listening to you.

Enjoy the Lord's awareness of you. The love of God enfolds you. Your concerns are being respected.

The patience of God is infinite. There are no sins, no habits, or inclinations that cannot be redeemed. God rewards us with blessings beyond our imagination. The advice of the apostle Paul needs repeating. I Thessalonians 5:16. We can learn to rejoice despite our moods and feelings. Rejoicing is a way of practicing mind over matter.

We need to give ourselves permission to enjoy ourselves as we notice and delight in the many gifts that God showers on us each day.

Act the way you really want to be. In a brief moment, you will become exactly the way you act. We create expectations of ourselves to gain a life-giving attitude that will be the foundation of how we act.

The Holy Spirit will give us the fruit of the Spirit so we will discover the delight that is possible. People cling to the status quo. They refuse to believe that prayer helps. Of course, as one of my critics insists, "God helps those who help themselves."

When our times of praying and walking with God, we know we have a companion even if we feel that we are alone. God is the silent voice we hear in our darkness.

Our prayer is a simple request. We ask God to remind us that we have not been abandoned to wander forever alone. This is often a flicker in our soul.

It is that tiny voice within that says, "You are always loved." Our journey demands we continue to lighten our load. Let go of the illusions, attitudes, relationships, and those things that prevent us from being one with God.

We come face to face with our shadows and our fears. Layer by layer, our illusions turn to reality. We simply begin to see more clearly.

When we hear music that moves us to tears. We hear the wordless language of rhythm and melody. Deep inside, we hold a profound longing for God. Listen for the music. The music inspired by God reveals the deep longing that God has for us.

God hungers for union with us in unlimited love. We were made in the likeness and image of God. The journey of our soul is to go back to God without shame knowing we are loved.

My loyal readers, the journey you take is uniquely yours. It is yours like the circles around a stone dropped into a creek or skipped to the other side. The love, grace, and forgiveness we give ripples to the waters of someone's life.

The spiritual path is not a straight line, but a uniquely winding road. Sip this book slowly. Walk inside my words and discover the places where it leads you to go.

Our faithfulness in prayer brings moments when the Holy Spirit has been preparing in me "beneath the surface" and blossoms. If intimate prayer is followed, we will know God's purpose. Prayer brings our souls, minds, and wills into communion with the will of Christ.

Sometimes God gives us unusual insight and times of loving kindness as we mysteriously have communion with the saints in heaven.

More than 25 years have passed since I had the privilege of studying at the University of Oxford. I stayed in Christ Church College in the room of a building where John Wesley had lived. One day following a class lecture, I had an unusual spiritual experience.

I was feeling a single-minded love of Jesus. As I walked into the room where Wesley had slept and worked, where he had prayed, and where he and others were made fun of and were called Methodists because of their disciplined lifestyle. While standing there in his room, I was moved to knell in prayer. I remembered how Wesley had struggled here after he had his heart "strangely moved" as evidence of the joy of his salvation. After his graduation from the University of Oxford, he traveled to Georgia to serve as a missionary. His ministry there was a complete failure. As a 36-year-old, he fell in love with a teen-aged young woman with whom he was aloft, but visibly stricken. He was driven out of Georgia, and traveled by ship with some Moravians who led him into has conversion experience.

The Holy Spirit was showing me that the most important thing about John Wesley was that he loved Jesus. Jesus lived deeply within Wesley. I began to feel Wesley's presence. I felt that he was praying for me. Wesley is with Jesus now and with us as an elder brother. I am now a retired elder in the Holston Conference of the United Methodist Church, denomination founded by the Wesleyan movement.

Chapter Ten

The Music of Kindness

When I think of the broad issue of kindness, I think of the words of Saint Augustine, "Joy is music of the soul." Kindness is one of the notes played in the music of living. To enjoy life a little more is the best way to spend your precious life. If I can give encouragement and support to just one reader, I think I have succeeded as minister of joy to the world.

Kindness and joy go hand in hand. Kindness is the oil that helps us to bear discomfort for the sake of all we love. I realize that I have been one instrument of the symphony of the Holy Spirit when people contact me to say they enjoyed and found help in one of my sermons or books.

I have purchased thousands of dollars' worth of my own books to give away to family and friends. My work has now been translated into many languages. A Pakistani Christian had it published in her country. People contact me to say that each book blesses them in differing ways.

In this book about the fruit of kindness, I have attempted to go beyond the material covered in previous books. Graduation from high school, college, and seminary bought me human joy for a while, but the thrill soon passes.

Love takes courage as well as faith. My goal in writing this book and having it published is to help the readers realize Jesus' goal for us all, "that your joy may be full."

Jesus possessed the Spirit of Joy. We are to imitate Jesus. I Thessalonians 5:16. God offers eternal joy. We do not have to wait until we reach heaven to enjoy life.

Getting closer to the Holy Spirit, we gain insight. Wordless prayer gives it to us. The spirit gets us out of ourselves. After my brother David died, I saw in his home that he collected our family photographs. Seeing myself as an infant was like an out-of-body experience. My tiny body no longer exists. I know my adult body will disappear.

That child in the picture has now become old, past 80. All the cells in that baby's body have changed. They changed every seven years. Part of me disappears every day.

My soul has remained basically the same. That body no longer exists, but I do. I am still here. When I served as chaplain and substance abuse counselor at Valley Hope Treatment Centers in Nebraska, one of my recovering alcoholic shared his conversion story. His insight moment came as he prayed to God in the rain. He was sick, homeless, still drinking. He said that he cried out, "This is not who I am. This is not what God placed in this world to be."

Our souls remain static because of our body cravings. Moments of awareness change our lives. This present world will pass away. Kindly remember that in Christ, we are destined for glory.

I keep scrapbooks of the times when I felt that I was successful in the world's eyes. They are only snapshots of my passing life. Everything changes. The past can never be lived again. Everything changes.

In this moment we might be at the top of the heap, but tomorrow you might hit the bottom. Success and failure are passing things. The real you that is living in your mind, body, spirit, and soul lives through all the seasons of our lives. (James McReynolds, *Joy in the Seasons of Life*, pp. 1-108.)

Unless we take control of our thoughts, life becomes miserable. Those who identify with negative thoughts and feelings are vulnerable to mental illness.

When I express negative thoughts or unkind interpretations of my past seasons of life, I have tried to say to myself that I am not alone. God is with me all the time. I am not filled with fear for God is my strength. I have been forgiven all my sins with God's loving kindness. I am bearing good fruits.

The Holy Spirit gives us the power to wipe out negative thinking. I no longer believe that I am unattractive, unloved, or just not adequate. No matter, keep loving yourself. Even if it seems that the whole world is irked with you. Those you counted on are now gone away.

The situation will change. The current time will pass. Magic from ordinary people will return. You will be connected again.

Cherish each moment. Stop waiting for that one perfect moment that will change your life. An Arizona cactus blooms only one time in a year. The plant does not consider the rest of its time as wasted. All moments count. Quiet moments. Boring moments. Sharing moments. Exciting moments. Each moment in time is equally important. Our now moments bring transformation.

It is a waste of energy to hold on to the past. By the moment that we reach toward it, it's gone. Stay in the present moment, the frame you are in right now. That's the only moment where loving kindness and joy can be found.

We are a Temple of the Holy Spirit.

Filling the soul with the Holy Spirit will help you through the trials much easier. Many women identify with their bodies. These women will always see flaws. A woman is not her body. She lives in her body that changes all the time. Her soul is filled with a spirit. Ladies, pray for the Holy Spirit to flood your soul with blessings. Males, too, must do the same.

God crafted us s integrated beings of mind, body, and soul to serve as the temples of the Holy Spirit. The English word "temple," refers to the consecrated ground as the building built for the worship of God. First Corinthians 3:17.

As we grow older, we now own old temples, but good ones. The biblical record tells us a man named Methuselah lived 969 years. Genesis 5:27.
We look forward to eternal life. And we hope to enjoy a long life as wayfarers here on earth. It is impossible and unlikely that we could live 969 years, the pursuit of longevity honors the Holy Spirit who lives in our bodies. If we live more than 80 years, we are far above the average.

We have no inkling when our own judgment day will come. We want to turn our long lifestyle into a long health span.

A human temple, regardless of how small, how large, how misshapen, how shaky, or how crooked are the creation of God. My brother-in-law Roger is 90 years old. He is short, half blind, had five bypasses in his heart and a pig valve, and he suffers from seizures. Bodies, intellects, and wills were created in the image of God. God loves us with infinite, loving kindness regardless of what our bodies look like.

Each person is unique. In loving kindness we delight in the wonder and miracle of the human body. God accepts all the broken pieces we offer. Luke 10:27. Love yourself. Remember that Jesus lives in you, in the temple of the body. Pray. Meet God there in your mind, in your body, and in your soul. First Corinthians 3:16-17, 6:19-20.

Believing in Christ, when it comes to our bodily temples, the best is yet to come. Even the bodies with significant disabilities will receive perfected bodies restored in heaven, and they will fly like eagles and walk without being weary.

Paying attention to our temples while we live on earth prepares us for our future glorified bodies. We are grateful for our bodily temples as we rest in hope of new glorified ones.

Live in the now. We are much more than our present state of mind might indicate. Bad things will happen in every life, but they need not undermine our confidence in the love and grace of God.

Nothing is as it appears. That goes for our beginning, our past, present, and future. Do not drag the past and your guilty and negative feelings into the present moment.

We are not our body. We are not the person in our baby pictures. You are not your past. We need to respect ourselves. We are our best friend. Love everything about yourself, body, mind, and soul. Live in wholeness. God believes that your temple of the spirit is beautiful.

By working on conditioning our minds and memory in these ways, we will be willing to live in the present moment. Enjoy God's loving kindness will give us the power to take control of our lives. Enjoy God more. Experience that God is enjoying your company and mine.

Heaven is our goal. We will have to keep on transforming ourselves to arrive there. We will continue to live in mystery, and God will give us the gift of wisdom.

Wherever you are, listen for the music. We are invited to join in. Do not fear to join in. Don't just stand quietly in the shadows watching other enjoy the music. Once Laurel and I went to a party where the people were doing karaoke. I joined in and sang "Rocky Top" and some Elvis Presley songs.

Some of my enjoyable moments came during my wife's church choir Christmas party in our home. Laurel played her piano with people we both cherish and love.

Drink in the kindness. Live in a joyful presence. Be a minister of joy to the world. Each of us is one tiny instrument in the symphony that plays kind and joyful songs.

God loves us. Delight in us is God's character. When we sing, our songs are deep in mystery. We see through a glass darkly when we sing of our faith in a thousand languages. Singing keeps us locked in the present moment. We cast aside memories and bad feelings that surround them. Your past cannot bring you down. Stay in the present moment. Receive the gift of joy from Jesus. The sounds of music can be healing. Music is in the voice of a friend. It sounds in the laughter of a child. Even sounds of silence are not silent. Each creation sings its own song. It requires a quiet mind, a quiet soul, and a quiet heart to hear these songs. Silence sings a beautiful song.

Music is all around us. Listen to its comforting sounds. Don't worry about how you can carry a tune. Sing along for a moment of joy in your life. Sing Joy to the World. Remind yourself how much you have been blessed. I enjoy reading my own books when I am down, sad, or depressed. The music that brings joy to you. Jesus came to earth to bring joy to the world. John 14:11. Go with me as we serve as ministers of joy to the world.

Once we discover the spiritual connection between love and joy, we can begin to enjoy life fully. Experience joy. We must bring love, grace, joy, and kindness to the surface. It takes faith and faithfulness to cooperate with the plan of God of bringing joy to the world.

Exercise your joy muscles. Cast aside past memories and lock yourself into the present time. Stay in the moment. Control your thoughts. Invite joy into your conscious mind. Become a messenger of joy to the world.

By conditioning your mind and memory, you will be willing to live in the present moment. Negative thoughts and desires will lose the power they have had over you.

A successful musician finds her bliss in performing with musical skills and continuous practice.

You will enjoy the Lord of your precious life more than ever. And God will continue to enjoy you. You will experience loving kindness and joy wherever you go. This is God's plan for you.

Joy Is Our Next Lesson.

Learning loving kindness, love, and joy is your next lesson. Being joyful is our mission. Learning to be and do kind has been difficult. For us to give compassionate kindness for others without judging, we had to go through difficult times ourselves.

Despite our best efforts, we could not help ourselves. Searching and searching in every division of our life, no answers came.

Understanding love has taken us many years. We have experienced many heartbreaks and grasping until we discovered the key to unconditional love was right inside of us.

Understanding joy is the foundation for our next life lesson. Go where the joy is. Do not ever stop. Don't give up. Do not let the pain and residue from the early parts of your journey stop you from going forward.

Do not tell yourself that the way you feel indicates that you can just stop. It is the way every one of us feels, who is committed to climbing and moving mountains.

Never stop. Relax as possible. Your rhythm of life is still here and now. Focus intently on each step. Soon you will reach just where you and God want you to be.

Soon, you shall reach your goal. You will find unbelievably joy. Keep your eyes focused on the path. Hold your head up. Look straight ahead. Embrace the thrill of your journey.

Fall in love with your destiny. Searching outside ourselves for some exclusive moment, we think we should go to be somewhere other than where we are. We would like to be someone else. We imagine that all our friends and those we encounter complain and regret their past.

Fall in love with your own life. Our destiny is not in some far-off moment or something that happens to somebody else. Your destiny is taking place right now. It is a mysterious energy or force that weaves things to create your personal destiny.

Love all the places you have gone. Anticipate more joy as you visit places in the rest of your years.

Most of all, love where you are now. That is where your destiny lies.

I know that you have worked and put effort into your own responsibility. Now reach out for your surprising yet anticipated rewards. Now is the time for you to know joy.

Acknowledge the traumatic events did happen. It was not your fault. You are not responsible. Reclaim your control. Feelings of helplessness carry into adulthood. You may feel and act like a perpetual victim. The past is in control of the present.

Seek support. Do not isolate yourself. Withdrawing from others will only make things worse. Take care of your health. Get plenty of rest. Eat well with healthy food. Practice and accept your reality. That does not mean that you have to embrace the trauma. Let it go. Decide what you will do with it. With God and the Spirit of Joy, we can do the impossible.

As my teacher and friend wrote, "If you learn to live this way every day, you will always have a song in your heart and the path before you will be lined with flowers. Joy will spring up inside you like a fountain, and you will lie down to sleep at night with peace in your soul. And you will say, 'Blessed be the name of our God forever and forever, who calls us to a new rule where righteousness will be the order of the day forever.'" (John Killinger, *Letting God Bless You: The Beatitudes for Today*, p. 139)

Chapter 11

The Memories of Unkindness

I came into this world during the time of World War II. My daddy was fighting the Japanese in Iwo Jima and Saipan. He was gone from the home through that time until the end of the war.

I recall very little about my childhood. I recall my mother and her sister yelling at each other. About the age of two, I recall pulling a cabinet of dishes over and the pain and blood involved.

Some of my friends' fathers never came home from the war. Some funerals were held across the street from the one-room apartment that was up over a grocery store at Woodlawn Baptist Church. I only remember the anxiety and all that goes with losing a father.

My mom and dad had traumatic childhoods. That trauma was never resolved. It passed from my parents to me and my siblings. Sadly, it went from unconscious mind to unconscious mind. Children are vulnerable. My parents lived out their trauma. It was too much for my brother and me. When things got wild, we would go into the Stone Castle or the Bristol Memorial Stadium to hide out.

The war had affected every soldier in traumatic ways. My father rarely talked about it. He kept his war medals on a wall until he died.

These sources of trauma and their effects live on if they are unresolved. They affected my youth and adult years in many forms and many ways. My childhood friends and I played war games. We had many plastic soldiers and tanks, ships, Ryder

BB guns, and we watched war movies from the wars with native Americans on into Vietnam and our recent wars.

My trauma lives inside of me. I have no power to help another person get healed from their trauma, but I have the possibility of healing on my own. My anger and stress from the past pops out from almost anything. These little moments serve as a subtle reminder of what happened to me as a child.

We and those close to us live with the upsurges of symptoms that leak out under stress or unpleasant reminders. People do heal from unresolved childhood drama.

If you experienced childhood drama, it comes as a surprise that the problems will raise their ugly heads when you become an adult. My personal child and youth trauma has ruined my happiness, my relationships, and my professional areas.

I often feel lost. Not seen. Not heard. Pushed aside. Left out. I push my own needs aside. My parents remained unreachable throughout my life. I never felt heard, seen, held, emotionally embraced, or valued. This has been there for my entire existence.

I became wary of my needs and uncertainty about being loved. So I learned to stay distant. From age 18 on, I left home every summer to serve as a summer home missionary for my Baptist church. I found that preaching revivals and conducting Vacation Bible Schools in places distant from my home fulfilled many of my needs.

I have remained too perfectionistic. I have tried to please, but I have never felt good enough. I always worried about being different. I am not socially confident. I am never sure where I fit in.

Losing a parent to abandonment or death is a trauma. My dad lost his dad when he was but eight years old. No matter how nurtured you were by your other relatives or the remaining parent, the loss remains deep in your soul.

Unresolved childhood trauma affects self-esteem and creates anxiety. All trauma is technically in the past. They live on in your current experiences, symptoms, and relationships. The roots of the past are still alive in the present. Now. Your childhood drama remains unresolved.

I often feel like remaining in a shell. I begin to be anxious again. There is only so much I can do by myself. I think the symptoms are gone, but they continue to go underground. When memories and flashbacks return, the only option is to cut them off. Tell yourself to just forget.

Keep your feelings a secret even from yourself. Childhood trauma is quite complex. I have never admitted that my childhood pastor sexually abused me. I still have many of the books and ministry materials that he gave me.

Perhaps that is one reason I have experienced so much pain from the church. I always hope my next parish will be the perfect one. No one ever talked to me about this. Those who have hurt me told me it would be best if I never tell anyone.

As I have kept quiet, I stayed embarrassed and ashamed. I did not think it should bother me. I also do not believe that I should be suffering now. Forgetting was the only option I thought I had.

I might be an adult, an old one, but my child self still lives inside. That child lives in our feelings and in our memories. My past lives on. I have tried everything possible to build a good and flourishing life in spite of it.

I have finally found love after many relationships. I love and feel loved by my wife and my family. I think I have created a successful career.

Our Past Waits for Reminders

The past lives on inside waiting for reminders. Although it is not fair, our past lies in wait for something to bring it up. Forgetting does not work for me. I need continued help for the triggers will not keep quiet.

I know I have dreams, symptoms, and feelings. These may be messages that I need to hear. Realizing that I remain hurt, and suffering. is not a bad thing. Now I have a new opportunity to know more about my suffering. I am not to blame, but I remain responsible.

It is not too late. We can always change. Don't keep your feelings secret or live with them alone. The right therapist can guide you. Remember not any therapist has the ability or experience in healing childhood trauma.

Some people have plenty of memories from various stages of early life. Others remember little or nothing about the formative years. They search and search their brains but come up with nothing more than fuzzy images.

Childhood amnesia or the loss of memories from the first several years of life is quite normal. Helping people regain so-called repressed memories is unethical.

I personally struggle with memories that have an emotional component. I sometimes think it is strange that people cannot remember certain key events that parents have told them about. Never suggest that we should remember these things as they remember them.

Memories are not supposed to become permanent. Please realize that many memories will fade away. We have a stronger capacity for memory as an adult, but we will still not remember everything.

Memories of childhood generally begin fading as we come into early adolescence. Having no childhood memories frustrates us. We think our memories are just lurking under the surface, just out of reach. Some researchers have concluded that memories do not completely disappear.

Talking about things we do remember with our loved ones. We should ask them questions to add substance to our tiny glimpses of memory.

We resist using the word surrender. We hold these negative nuances that distort the significance of letting go. Surrender actually carries a richer reality. We are able to receive a loving kindness that is beyond our imaginations. This is the key to receiving what we want.

We struggle with the paradoxes of life. We think there are no answers, no rational explanations, and the mysteries that exceed our human understanding. We are trying to hold everything together. We want to be in control of ourselves facing things that cannot really be explained. We honestly want to do something.

Surrender is not a submissive defeat. The paradox of letting go into forgiveness and love frees us to walk with renewed life. Our reward is the energy that exceeds our vision and the freedom to walk in joy.

When loved ones need us with their losses and pains, we are good at "being there." We graciously stand by them in supporting kindness. We pray that someone will be willing to sit with us when it's our time.

We sometimes attempt to fill the hollow place where we are living in the present moment. Eventually, we must name the facts and the feelings that are ours. We are the only ones, besides God, who can hear our souls.

We need outside witnesses and supportive others to be with us. We sit with ourselves on the dark shore. We must be the voice that we hear in our bed at night that tells us we will be fine, and that God will never abandon you. Give yourself a dose of wordless kindness.

Some of us have known the immense Mystery of God that holds us in our moments of distress. We continue to ask for the loving kindness to fill the space as we mindfully, gently, and kindly listen to the songs in our soul.

We touch the loving kindness of God, who gives us the words our spirit so longs to hear. The judgments will melt away in the waves of kindness. Then, we will extend our kindness to others. We will graciously rest in the promises of God. Emptiness will make way for fullness.

The paradox of the beatitudes reminds us that emptiness makes way for fullness. We are most deeply connected with God in our souls. The healing connection is a wordless place of simply knowing what we know. We hold waves of insight.

God invites us to enter soul-waters and to surrender to the unconditional love of God that has always supported us. That is all we need to continue our journey.

Keeping Track of Our Memories

Keep track of what you do remember. Write it down with as much detail as possible. Keep a private journal of your memories. Add details later if they come to you.

Childhood photographs could help you recapture early memories. Perhaps you received a small train on your second birthday. Your parents will probably be astonished that you have completely forgotten.

When glancing through old photos, focus on those from everyday life. Memories of things that happened regularly are stronger than memories of one-time or rare events.

Going back to the scenes from your childhood evoke some forgotten memories. As you walk down familiar streets and even notice certain smells, these trigger moments from your past.

Much in my hometown, Bristol, Tennessee-Virginia has changed in the former neighborhood. The house my dad built at 1300 Edgemont Avenue is no longer there. My Tennessee High School constructed Viking Hall, a spacious place for sports and graduations, where our home once stood.

Lifelong learning can strengthen the brain. Brain training will not enable us to recall any childhood memories. Doing puzzles and watching games shows will not hurt. It could trigger those memories that you still have.

Both mental exercises and regular physical activity will have a positive impact on not just your memory, but your brain health overall.

Living through a traumatic childhood or living through one that was perfectly pleasant will make little difference. Most forget the memories in the normal course of development. This normality includes unsettling gaps in your memory. Notice memories that conflict with what others have told you about the past. Of course, there will be strong negative emotions attached to specific memories.

The treatment that I have benefited from has been to identify the triggers, to develop coping strategies, and decrease the symptoms. I have tried to work on myself in supportive and safe environments.

Kindness and empathy is strongly needed as the stigma of mental health hurts chances of survival. Military people often shun any diagnosis that infers that the military personnel are not perfect.

Trauma has consequences that continue into adulthood. Some of these conditions include eating disorders, substance and alcohol disorders, major depressive disorders, PTSD, and suicide.

Go Where the Joy Is.

Go where the joy is and enjoy every drop of love that you deserve. Forgiveness and loving kindness are the only way we can move forward. Some people conceive forgiveness as the willingness to see beyond what has been done to us.

The struggle to forgive includes our attitudes and behaviors from learning to live with memories of the past to coping with feelings of resentment and even desires for vengeance, to loving our enemies, and being examples of reconciliation.

We will have to pray with energy and for a long time to experience the grace of forgiveness. The Holy Spirit is our guide here. With the Spirit, we are able to move past our human natures with miracles. Grace allows us to make choices and tapping into the Spirit of peace and joy.

Forgiveness is the most important action. We need to forgive others and our need to feel forgiveness. Failing to forgive others brings about the danger of our alignment with negative forces.

Forgive all adversaries quickly. The first step in forgiveness is overcoming resentment. We must learn to like someone that we never liked before. By showing kindness, you accept your own will to love.

We will be blessed in ways we never anticipated. Keep alert for both expected and unexpected results of our prayer.

The gift of forgiveness is a gift for me as well as the one forgiven. Forgiveness brings freedom for ourselves. This is how we get unstuck. Getting used to feeling stuck will bring nothing but more pain.

Even though forgiving and being kind goes against our grain at first, when we practice with loving kindness toward those we believe are to blame, forgiveness begins to become possible.

It is an amazing surprise to me when a hurting person has now broken out of the trap of victimhood. They are the ones who in the strength of God, bring compassion and forgiveness to the who wronged them.

They transcend human and cultural expectation. They go deeper and they integrate and overcome what was clearly an injustice. Their vision quest becomes much larger than the wounded conception of the present situation.

There are rewards in the act of forgiveness and letting go. Your human arms will be free to receive the unconditional blessings, the grace gifts, and the love.

The flowers that my wife planted in her garden from seeds will be like new growth full of vitality that will be revealed. The flowers wait for their time to open up, to blossom and blaze brightly.

Bibliography

Ashman, John. *Quest: A Theology of Joy*. Halifax, Canada: Quest Publication, 2020.

Baskerville, Ken. "Reaction to Random Acts of Kindness," *The Social Science Journal*. 37, 293-298, 1981.

Binfet, John Tyler. "Not so Random Acts of Kindness: A Guide to Intentional Kindness," *The International Journal of Emotional Education*, Volume 7, Number 2, pp. 49-62, November 2015.

Brach, Tara. *Radical Acceptance: Embracing Your Life with the Heart*. New York: Bantam Dell, 2003.

Coakley, Sarah. *A New Asceticism: Sexuality, Gender, and the Quest for God*. New York: Bloomsbury, 2015.

Davis, M.H. "A Multidimensional Approach to Individual Differences in Empathy," *JSAS Catalogue of Selected Documents in Psychology*, 1985.

Donovan, Jill. *The Effect of Kindness*. Baltimore: Charisma House, 2018.

Edel, Lawrence. *Henry James: A Life*. New York: Harper Collins, 1987.

Gendler, J. Ruth. *The Book of Qualities*. Berkeley, California: Turquoise Mountain Publications, 1980.

Gorrell, Angela. *The Gravity of Joy*. Grand Rapids, Michigan: Eerdmans Publishing Company, 2020.

Hegarty, Patricia. *Books of Kindness*. New York: Penguin Random Books, 2023.

Jenson, David. *God, Desire, and a Theology of Human Sexuality.* Philadelphia: Westminster John Knox Press, 2013.

Johnson, Spencer. *The Present: The Secret to Enjoying Your Work and Life, Now.* New York: Doubleday and Random House, 2006.

Jones, Gregory. *Embodying Forgiveness: A Theological Analysis.* Grand Rapids, Michigan: William B. Eerdmans Publishing Company, 1998.

Killinger, John. *Letting God Bless You: Beatitudes for Today.* Nashville: Abingdon Press, 1992.

Killinger, John. *Lost in Wonder, Love, and Praise.* Nashville: Abingdon Press, 2001.

Killinger, John. *Rising Your Spiritual Awareness through 365 Simple Gifts from God.* Nashville: Dimensions for Living, 1998.

Koenig, Harold G. *The Healing Power of Faith:* New York: Simon and Shuster, 1999.

Lovasik, Lawrence G. *The Hidden Power of Kindness.* South Bend, Indiana: Sophia Institute Press, 2021.

Martin, Ralph. *Hungry for God: Practical Help in Personal Prayer.* Cincinnati, Ohio: Saint Anthony Messenger Press, 2007.

McLaren, Brian D. *Way of Life.* Nashville: Abingdon Press, 2017.

McReynolds, James. *Joy Beyond the Walls of This World: Healing the Souls of Men and Women.* Cleveland, Tennessee: Parson's Porch Books, 2021.

McReynolds, James. *Joy Filled Souls: It Is Well with My Soul.* Cleveland, Tennessee: Parson's Porch Books, 2022.

McReynolds, James. *Living the Dream: Adventure in Marriage.* Cleveland, Tennessee: Parson's Porch Books, 2021.

McReynolds, James. *Spirit of Joy Church.* Cleveland, Tennessee: Parson's Porch Books, 2019.

McReynolds, James. *The Joy of Prayer: The Way to Intimacy with God.* Cleveland, Tennessee: Parson's Porch Books, 2020.

McReynolds, James. *The Gospel of Joy: Global Impact of the Ministry of Joy to the World.* Cleveland, Tennessee: Parson's Porch Books, 2022.

McReynolds, James. *The Silence of the Church: The Spiritual Struggle with Sexuality.* Cleveland, Tennessee: Parson's Porch Books, 2017.

McReynolds, James. *The Strength of Being Tender: Love Is Like a Butterfly.* Cleveland, Tennessee: Parson's Porch Books, 2022.

Nevi, Judy. *All Kinds of Kindness.* New York: Simon and Schuster, 2022.

Otake, Ken and James Tanaka-Matsumi. "Happy People Become Happier Through Kindness: Accounting Kindness Intervention," *Journal of Happiness Studies,* 7, 361-375, 2020.

Reynolds, William J. *Joyful Sound.* New York: Holt, Rinehart, and Winston, 1978.

Salzberg, Sharon. *Lovingkindness: The Revolutionary Art of Happiness.*
Boston: Shambhala Press, 1995.

Santomero, Angela C. *Radical Kindness*. New York: Harper and Ware, 2020.

Saussy, Carroll. *The Art of Growing Old; a Guide to Faithful Aging*. Minneapolis: Augsburg Publishing Company, 1998.

Seidlitz, Lewis and Edward Diener, "Memory for Positive Versus Negative Life Events: Theories for the Differences Between Happy and Unhappy Persons," *Journal of Personality and Social Psychology*, 64, pp. 654-664, 1993.

Stoldt, April. *Share Some Kindness, Bringing Some Light*. New York: Simon and Schuster, 2022.

Watson, Christie. *The Language of Kindness: A Nurse's Story*. New York: Tim Duggan Books, imprint of Crown Publishing of Penguin Random House, 2020.

Webber, Robert E. *God Still Speaks: A Biblical View of Christian Communication*. Nashville: Thomas Nelson Publishing Company, 1980.

Weiss, Andrew. *Beginning Mindfulness*. Novato, California: New World Library, 2004.

Wesley, John. *A Collection of Hymns for the People Called Methodists*. London, England: Unpublished lyrics housed in the museum of Wesley Chapel, 1759.

About the Author

Jim is just an ordinary person who has lived with painful situations in these fractured times. Like his readers, he has had to endure negative habits, flawed thoughts, and unkindness from culture that holds no empathy. He has done the work of forgiveness for his sins and the sins of others.

The loving kindness and grace of God has been working with the Holy Spirit to bring his soul the power to change including inner healing, growth, and maturity.

As people begin to know Jim, they share his warmth. Sitting on the porch and sharing a cup of tea, watching birds, eating chocolate, burning incense, or fresh air brings out a mutual connection.

As the Minister of Joy to the World, he calls himself a joyologist. A joyologist is a person who studies joy and shares it with the world. The author was introduced to a serious study of joy in a doctoral seminar on joy at the Vanderbilt University Divinity School in Nashville, Tennessee.

Nothing is more difficult than having to release a dream, a habit, a thing, or a person that we have cherished. God provides all our needs, including other ordinary people who have shown extraordinary kindness.

My readers and friends, family, and colleagues face what they perceive as impossibilities. Life brings us into situations where their seems no way out. Difficult people and awesome opportunities confront every one of us.

Most of us live our lives within the narrow limits of what we can do on our own strength. Problems, challenge, and opportunities that we can't avoid. I shared these thoughts with my congregation, the First Presbyterian Church in Tecumseh,

Nebraska. Each of us was to think about their lives and the unlimited power of God. We were to also see where we had stepped back from being involved in something that we could not do by ourselves. We were then to visualize a difficult relationship, illness, limitation, crisis that we had kept away from, because we wanted to keep life safe and free of risk. John 14:12-14.

On time and in time God invades our problems with extraordinary power.
There are times when God brings those problems before us so we can be astounded with what is done with the impossibilities. Keep that vision focused on your mind.

All that this writer writes in this book will make more sense if readers keep their God-directed impossibility before us. It is God who gives us our impossible dream. If you think you have lost your dream, Jim has created a blueprint for loving kindness.

He takes time to express himself every day by writing, painting, preaching to bring something beautiful into the world. God inspires his creativity. This creative book offers ways to activate joy in surprising moments. Joy is essential for nourishing the mind, the body, heart, and soul.

There has been times when he has had to relinquish control of his family, or profession, or a perceived future to be called back to the realization that they are not his, but a gift from God that is held in trust.

We now live in the Lord's loving kindness assures us that in the right time, God will resurrect all our impossibilities which we have surrendered. Jim infuses a sudden spark of divine energy. He desires to share his wisdom and heartfelt connection to those he encounters.

This book is a gift of loving kindness to place powerful cement into your fractures to bring the joy of the Lord.

During the peak moments, the author knows a fullness in which life is positive, meaningful, and worth being lived. Loving kindness is associated with meeting others and sharing a positive expeience.